No Place For Violence

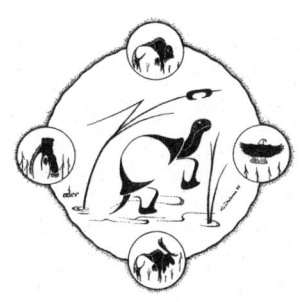

No Place For Violence
Canadian Aboriginal Alternatives

Edited by Jocelyn Proulx and Sharon Perrault

**Co-published by Fernwood Publishing
and RESOLVE** (Research and Education for Solutions to Violence and Abuse)

Copyright © 2000 Jocelyn Proulx and Sharon Perrault

All rights reserved. No part of this book may be reproduced or transmitted in any form by any means without permission in writing from the publisher, except by a reviewer, who may quote brief passages in a review.

Editing: Eileen Young
Images: George Delorme
Design and production: Beverley Rach
Printed and bound in Canada by: Hignell Printing Limited

A publication of:
Fernwood Publishing
Box 9409, Station A
Halifax, Nova Scotia
B3K 5S3
and
RESOLVE
(Research and Education for Solutions to Violence and Abuse)

Fernwood Publishing Company Limited gratefully acknowledges the financial support of the Department of Canadian Heritage and the Canada Council for the Arts for our publishing program.

Canadian Cataloguing in Publication Data

Main entry under title:

No place for violence

Includes bibliographical references.
ISBN 1-55266-034-6

1. Family violence -- Canada -- Prevention. 2. Indians of North America -- Canada -- Social conditions. I. Perrault, Sharon. II. Proulx, Jocelyn

HV6626.23.C3N6 2000   362.82'92'08997071   C00-950119-3

Contents

Acknowledgements 9
About the Authors 10

Chapter 1: Introduction
Sharon Perrault and Jocelyn Proulx 13
    Aboriginal Values: People and Community 13
    Colonization and the Aboriginal Community 15
    Family Violence and Aboriginal People 16
    Community Response 17
    Current Needs in Dealing with Family Violence 19

Chapter 2: Could This Be Your Community?
Elizabeth Thomlinson, Nellie Erickson and Mabel Cook 22
    The Background 22
        Initiating the Current Study 24
        Reported Cases of Family Violence 24
    Survey of Unreported Cases 25
        Method 25
        Results 27
    Discussion and Recommendations 34
    Conclusion 37

Chapter 3: "Everybody had black eyes": Intimate Violence, Aboriginal Women and the Justice System
Anne McGillivray and Brenda Comaskey 39
    Introduction 39
    Manitoba Justice Policy 40
    Intimate Violence and Aboriginal Women 41

    The Study 43
    The Participants 44
    Experiences of Violence 44
    Coping with Violence 47
    Police Response 47
    Justice System Response 49
    Jail or Diversion? 51
Reflections 53

Chapter 4: Aboriginal Ganootamaage Justice Services of Winnipeg (AGJSW)

Kathy Mallet, Kathy Bent, and Wendy Josephson 58
Introduction 58
History of Aboriginal Ganootamaage
Justice Services of Winnipeg 60
Aboriginal Ganootamaage Justice Services
of Winnipeg Staff 61
    The Board of Directors 61
    The Broken-Spirited Relations 61
    The Crown 62
    Aboriginal Court Workers 62
    The Community Council 63
    The Community Council Coordinator (CCC) 63
    The Elder 64
Aboriginal Ganootamaage Justice Services
of Winnipeg Process 65
    The Aims 65
    Developing Trust 66
    The Healing Plan 68
    Traditional Healing 69
    Circles—The Heart of AGJSW 70
    Other Traditional Ceremonies 73
    The Volunteer Program 73
    Public Education Component 74
Conclusion 75

Chapter 5: Striving Towards Balance: A Blended Treatment/Healing Approach with Aboriginal Sexual Offenders
Lawrence Ellerby 78
    The Evolution of the Blended Approach 79
    Expanding Paradigms: Holism, Wellness
    and Spirituality 81
    Delivering A Blended Treatment/Healing Model 82
        The Helpers 82
        The Clients 84
    The Modalities of the Blended Program 85
    The Teachings in a Blended Program 88
    The Continuum and Connectedness of Care 94
    Challenges of a Blended Treatment/Healing Model 95
    Benefits of a Blended Treatment/Healing Model 97

Chapter 6: The Ma Mawi Wi Chi Itata Stony Mountain Project: Blending Contemporary and Traditional Approaches for Male Family Violence Offenders
Jocelyn Proulx and Sharon Perrault 99
    Institutional Abuse of Aboriginal People 100
    Childhood Abuse and Family Violence Offenders 102
    The Cycle of Violence 104
    The Need for Aboriginal Specific Programming 104
    The Ma Mawi Wi Chi Itata Family Violence Program—
    Stony Mountain Project 106
    Community Reintegration 110
    Evaluation of the Stony Mountain Project 111
    Expansion of the Stony Mountain Family
    Violence Program 116
    Conclusion 118

Conclusion
Sharon Perrault and Jocelyn Proulx 120

References 128

Dedication

We dedicate this volume to all Aboriginal communities whose determination is to heal from the effects of violence. It is hoped that continued efforts will be made to search for alternatives to deal with concerns of justice and violence. Only then will we expand the possibilities to end the destruction that violence has inflicted on our communities and daily lives.

Acknowledgements

We gratefully acknowledge all of those individuals who have contributed to the publication of this volume. The diligent work of those on the series committee: Dr. Caroline Piotrowski, Dr. Wendy Josephson, Ms. Maria Wasylkewycz, Ms. Christine Ateah, and Ms. Sharon Perrault, who were responsible for the conceptualization of the series and this volume. RESOLVE provided the support and expertise in community/academic family violence research partnerships that was necessary to the formalization of this partnership within a series of research based volumes. We appreciate and admire the creativity and thoughtfulness of the artist who has designed the art work for the cover of the volume.

There are a number of individuals at Fernwood Publishing whose efforts were essential to the final product: Wayne Antony, managing editor; Eileen Young, copy editor for the volume; Debbie Mathers, typist of the final manuscript; Tim Dunn, proofreader; Beverley Rach, book design and layout.

As both editors and contributors to the volume, we recognize the courage and perseverance of all those who seek the path of healing. Ultimately, we must acknowledge the teachings and legacy that the Creator has given Aboriginal people throughout the world, including those within our own western Canadian region.

About the Authors

Kathy Bent is a psychology honours student at the University of Winnipeg whose research interests pertain to developmental, social and socio-cultural psychological issues. She has conducted research on the effects of Aboriginal cultural enrichment programs on female adolescent parents' self-perception.

Brenda Comaskey is Research Associate at RESOLVE (Research and Education for Solutions to Violence and Abuse). She completed her Bachelor of Arts (Advanced) and Master of Arts degrees at the University of Manitoba. With Anne McGillivray, she is co-author of *Black Eyes All of the Time: Aboriginal Women, Intimate Violence and the Justice System*.

Mabel Cook lives and works on Mosakahiken Cree Nation in Moose Lake, Manitoba. She is currently the administrative assistant at Rod Martin School and is the community Magistrate. Ms Cook has focused on prevention of abuse and violence within Aboriginal communities, particularly working with young people.

Lawrence Ellerby, Ph.D., is the Clinical Director of the Native Clan Organizations Forensic Behavioral Management Clinic in Winnipeg. The clinic provides institutional and community-based assessment and treatment services for sexual offenders. Dr. Ellerby is also the Canadian representative on the Board of Directors for the Association of the Treatment of Sexual Abusers.

Nellie Erickson, R.N., has nursed in northern Manitoba in acute care, long term care, community health and nursing administration. Her focus has been to work toward improving health services for Aborigi-

About the Authors

nal people in northern Manitoba. She has participated in education and research programs to improve the health of community members.

Wendy Josephson, Ph.D., is an Associate Professor of Psychology at the University of Winnipeg. She is a social psychologist whose research has been in the areas of media violence, domestic violence and dating violence prevention.

Kathy Mallett is the current Executive Director of Gannotamaage and has worked in the Aboriginal community for over twenty years. She is one of Winnipeg's most pro-active Aboriginal community leaders. She has contributed her extensive knowledge and experience in the areas of violence against women, education, housing, economic and community development, justice, child welfare and international solidarity to the Aboriginal community.

Anne McGillivray is a Professor of Law at the University of Manitoba. She has authored some forty articles, reviews, reports and edited collections on childhood rights, domestic violence and criminal justice, and law and literature. With Brenda Comaskey, she is co-author of *Black Eyes All of the Time: Intimate Violence, Aboriginal Women and the Justice System*.

Sharon Perrault is a Metis woman who has been vocal in promoting Aboriginal-specific programming and is an active participant in numerous academic and community research projects. She is the Central Site Manager of Ma Mawi Wi Chi Itata Inc., Team Leader of the Ma Mawi Wi Chi Itata Family Violence Program, and Associate Community Director for RESOLVE.

Jocelyn Proulx, Ph.D., is currently a Research Associate with RESOLVE. At the centre she has conducted several projects on a variety of family violence topics. Her current work is focused on family violence in the Aboriginal community and programming for Aboriginal inmates in federal institutions.

Elizabeth Thomlinson, R.N., Ph.D., is an assistant professor in the Faculty of Nursing at the University of Calgary. Dr. Thomlinson has practised nursing in rural and northern areas of Manitoba and on faculty at the University of Manitoba. Her research interests are children who are failing to thrive and their families, child abuse and neglect, and the roles and educational needs of nurses in rural and remote Canada.

Chapter 1

Introduction
Sharon Perrault and Jocelyn Proulx

Aboriginal Values: People and Community
Historically, Aboriginals are people of community (Lee, 1992). Marriages join bloodlines in a conjugal family that provides the social, political and spiritual basis for all of its members. Grandparents serve as the leaders in these families, setting behavioural and spiritual norms. The adoption of unrelated elders as grandparents in cases where natural grandparents are absent illustrates the importance of the grandparent role. A flexible and extensive family system is the standard (Herring, 1989). Children are taught and cared for within this extended family system. They are guided towards a community perspective and spirituality is integrated into their daily education and socialization. Naming ceremonies establish a network of community members who will care for children and take responsibility for raising them. Substitute parents are confirmed in the event the natural parents become unable to care for their children. Aboriginal communities generally are encouraged to take responsibility for each other. Children, in particular, are viewed as gifts from the Creator and alternatives are sought when the immediate family can no longer care for them. Thus, families extend through bloodlines, ceremonial practices, adoptions and affiliations.

Cooperation and a unity with nature are an essential part of Aboriginal culture. This unity with nature is an extension of the unity of each individual with their family and community. Time is part of this interconnectedness. Individuals are tied to their ancestors through time and receive direction from these spirit guides. Correspondingly, individuals are taught to weigh their actions carefully, as they will have an impact on subsequent generations

(Nabigon and Mawhiney, 1996). Intergenerational knowledge is sought and prioritized for the collective well-being of community members. Thus, regard for others extends well beyond the present.

Moreover, there is a respect for the role that all entities of nature play in the larger universe (Lee, 1992). All living things have a spirit and have values and wisdom to impart. For example, trees symbolize honesty and the variety of colours and sizes of people in the world. Animals teach affection, companionship and self-sacrifice for others. They also teach the value of sex and how not to abuse this activity (Nabigon and Mawhiney, 1996): two beings joining together is natural and profound and provides for the continuation and evolution of creation. The relationship with nature is equal and reciprocal; everything has a place in the world. Thought and consideration for all living things are balanced with respect for the intricacies of nature.

This interrelationship with all living things naturally extends to all peoples of the world. All humans are part of a global community. Just as people can learn from the natural aspects of their environments, they can learn from people of different races and cultures. This sense of worldwide community not only works to reduce racism and ethnocentrism and to generate the common values of wisdom, love, respect, honesty, kindness and truth, but it also works to negate the repetition of past human atrocities. More importantly, individuals learn to draw on each other's attributes, needs, values and similarities.

It is through the community and its teachings that individuals gain their sense of identity (Lee, 1992). A clear knowledge of where individuals come from, to whom they are related, and to which community they belong is essential to their concept of self and place in the universe. Recognition and balance of the aspects of personality are necessary characteristics of a healthy individual. The mental, physical, emotional and spiritual components of self must be integrated within the individual, just as individuals need to be integrated within families and communities, and in their relationship to the earth (Nabigon and Mawhiney, 1996). A positive sense of oneself and others is more easily achieved when living in a healthy environment.

In the Aboriginal concept, the features of personality are represented by the "hub"—a model of three concentric circles and four geographical directions (Nabigon and Mawhiney, 1996). The outer circle represents negative aspects of the self. The eastern direction of the outer circle represent feelings of inferiority and shame. These begin when, as children, individuals are made to feel powerless and victimized. To the south is envy, which reinforces feelings of inferiority and leads to unhappiness and discontent. Resentment and unspoken negative feelings, signified by the western direction, can accumulate and cause illness and a negative attitude. The northern direction represents apathy and a lack of care for oneself and others.

The inner circle represents positive elements of the self. The eastern direction signifies general well-being and positive emotion, including the elements that feed physical and spiritual well-being. These elements provide energy and enable individuals to cope with stress. The southern direction represents the ability to have positive relationships with oneself and others. The western direction signifies respect for self, others and all things on the earth. Respect requires that people consider the consequences of their behaviour before they act. In this way, they become responsive to the other entities with which they share the earth. The northern direction represents the act of caring for self and others.

The third, innermost circle is half darkness and half light. The dark half symbolizes jealousy, which fills a person with possessiveness and a sense of being unfulfilled. The light half is the spiritual fire of life's energy and the core energy of the individual. Thus, the inner and outer circles represent the means to heal and/or destroy. Perhaps it is the third circle which is most controversial, where the element of choice and opportunity exists. At this level individuals have the ability to enhance and heal themselves, their families and their communities. The challenge is to keep focused on the light in the circle and not become distracted or engulfed by the darkness.

Colonization and the Aboriginal Community

Colonization devastated the Aboriginal way of life at many levels and over several centuries. Military attacks against Aboriginal tribes were prevalent in the seventeenth and eighteenth centuries. These attacks destroyed families, communities, and in some cases, tribes. In the nineteenth century, Aboriginal people were settled on reserves, restricting their lives and movements. Their sense of global community was shattered. The twentieth century introduced institutionalization of Aboriginal children in residential schools and foster care. Removing these children from their families and communities and forbidding their traditional way of life prevented them from learning traditional values and cultural customs (Herring, 1989). They had no opportunity to be raised with an extended family and to develop a sense of unity with nature and other people of the earth.

Through colonization a new European individualistic perspective was imposed onto Aboriginal life. The cohesive aspects of Aboriginal life diminished as traditional customs and spirituality were forbidden. The collectives of family and community, and the sense of relationship with all people and all of nature were disrupted. The Elders' place in the community was negated through restrictions on cultural teachings. The extended family and sense of community was de-emphasized, while a focus on the nuclear family and individualism was accentuated. European ideas of the superiority of humans over all other living things was promoted. Moreover, Aboriginal women lost their place as decision makers and men became the dominant gender. Thus the balance of gender roles was interrupted and an aspect of Aboriginal life that had been revered for centuries disintegrated.

The effects of colonization continued into the twentieth century largely, but not only, through residential schools and institutionalized care. The movement of Aboriginal children from their homes into residential schools, and the mass placement of children in foster care and U.S. Caucasian adoptive homes during the 1960s and 1970s created a significant upheaval in the lives and development of Aboriginal children and families. Residential school and foster care placements took children away from their families and communities. Shame at being Aboriginal was instilled, as assimilation became the primary lesson taught in these institutions. Young minds were exposed to norms and values that further removed them from their community (Lee, 1992).

Family Violence and Aboriginal People

In recent years, family violence has become an issue of significant concern within the Aboriginal community. One of the unique aspects of family violence within this community is its link to the history of colonization. European ethnocentrism generated racist attitudes and discriminatory practices towards First Nations people. This racism is clear, for example, in the restriction of Aboriginal residences to reserves or to ghettos in Caucasian urban centres. Economic and social opportunities have been severely limited by both location and prejudice.

Aboriginal children who grew up in institutional care facilities such as residential schools suffered several forms of abuse. Psychological abuse occurred: speaking the language and following the traditions of their people were forbidden; they were forced to cut their hair; their names were changed and their characters maligned (Lee, 1992; McGillivray, 1997; Palmer and Cooke, 1996). Physical and sexual abuse was a common experience in residential schools; the extent of these abuses is only now being revealed.

Abuse, exposure to poor parenting models, and pervasive racism thus had severe adverse effects on the psychological and social functioning of many Aboriginal people. Their own lives became marked by violence and their children were often abused, neglected and sent into institutional care, thereby perpetuating a cycle of violence. Given the history of colonization, abuse and violence, it is not surprising that Aboriginal people represent approximately 15 percent of the federal offender population in Canada (Correctional Service Canada, 1999), 49 percent of inmates in Manitoba, 68 percent in Saskatchewan and 34 percent in Alberta (Griffiths and Verdun-Jones, 1994). These figures are far greater than the overall Aboriginal population across Canada (4 percent). This level of imprisonment only serves to further disrupt many Aboriginal lives, leaving a new generation of Aboriginal youth to carry the impact of this history into their adult lives.

Community Response

Efforts to address family violence often fail because they do not consider the role of culture. For Aboriginal people, a culturally-based response is necessary and such a response requires the "intervention" of the community. Just as the community nurtures its members to become healthy individuals, it can also guide them through the process of healing from violence. The Aboriginal community has been undermined, but it has never ceased to exist; recently it has become a stronger influence in the lives of its members.

Within the last decade, the Aboriginal community has become increasingly involved in addressing the pattern of abuse and violence. A number of Aboriginal agencies service the community with programs and shelters for women, children and men who have been affected by family violence. Some of the programs available are based on mainstream theories and methods while others are Aboriginal-specific. Still others offer a blend of mainstream and Aboriginal-specific approaches, presenting mainstream content through traditional teachings and ceremonies. This volume presents two examples of blended programming. Chapter 5 presents the Ma Mawi Wi Chi Itata Family Violence Program, a Winnipeg-based organization that provides blended programs for Aboriginal children, women and men within the community, and for Aboriginal men incarcerated at the Stony Mountain Federal Correctional Facility. Chapter 6 presents the work of the Native Clan Organization's Forensic Behavioral Management Clinic which provides a blended treatment program for Aboriginal sex offenders within the Winnipeg area.

Among the issues addressed in these programs are anger management, safety planning, parenting and sexuality. New more adaptive skills are taught in order to replace violent responses. Discussions of personal issues and experiences are typically conducted. In addition, there are often discussions of the effects of colonization: intergenerational abuse and dealing with racism. Aboriginal concepts of "Creator" and "Mother Earth" are used. The significance of these concepts and other Aboriginal teachings are part of the treatment process. Ceremonies such as sweat-lodges, smudges and feasts are incorporated into the process of support groups and individual counselling.

The goal of blended programs is to help victims and offenders regain a sense of balance within themselves. The inner self must become known and the inner core of spiritual fire kindled. For some, these programs are their first introduction to the idea of unity with nature and the global community, while others are reminded of the importance of this perspective. Part of the healing process is to acquire a balance with the various aspects of one's personality and with all other living things in the world. Re-establishing balance requires that those who did harm to others become part of the victim's healing. In this way the sense of community is not lost through the ostracism and isolation of some of its members. Chapter 4 of this volume presents a description of the Ganootamaage Justice Services of Winnipeg, an organization developed to provide alternative sentencing through the use of traditional and holistic Aboriginal methods for offenders who have committed non-violent crimes. The diversion program focuses on healing and restitution for both the offender and the victim. Thus, the victim is invited to be part of the offender's healing. It is believed that this traditional approach, which maintains the link between the offender and his or her community, will reduce isolation and provide the vehicle for finding a path of healing and community reintegration. It is the intent of these programs to generate attitudes of care, respect and empathy, thereby making the Aboriginal community stronger and healthier. Community-based programs provide individuals with the courage to face the pain they have caused and experienced, and to explore and understand their inner self. Healing from violence is a long-term process. The community provides the means and the support necessary to bring its members through that process.

The effects of colonization and racism has created a general need for healing among all Aboriginal people. Traditionally the community has come together to help its members heal. This process is being renewed through efforts to help Aboriginal people heal from violence. Culturally relevant programs reintroduce traditional methods to help individuals on the path of healing. These community-based efforts not only work to heal individuals, but allow the community to work together and heal as a whole, resulting in greater individual, family and community health.

Current Needs in Dealing with Family Violence

Despite current efforts, Aboriginal women and men have indicated that the response to family violence is still insufficient in a number of ways. First, the services for women and children need to be expanded to address the multidimensional nature of intergenerational abuse. There still exists a need to create more programs specifically designed for "women and anger." While men have been socialized to express their emotions through anger, women have been taught to suppress anger. This suppressed anger has claimed numerous female victims. Many have sought solace from their unexpressed anger by internalizing it, where it is manifested through depression, suicide, mental illness, substance abuse, eating disorders and other compulsive coping behaviours. Witnessing violence during childhood combined with socialization towards submissiveness has left many women vulnerable to becoming involved in violent relationships in their youth and adult lives.

As well, the lack of services in northern and rural communities is especially evident, as families in crisis must leave essential support systems and their homes to travel to urban areas to access services. While services for women and children are insufficient, the programs for Aboriginal men, even in urban areas, are even more limited. Chapter 2 of this volume presents research conducted in the northern communities of the Swampy Cree Tribal Council, Alberta. Community members identified a lack of information about family violence and a need for more services to address the problem of family violence, particularly in northern rural areas.

As with other social systems, the justice system's response to the needs of the Aboriginal community is being scrutinized. Chapter 3 of this volume explores the experience of Aboriginal female victims of family violence and their views of the response of the justice system to family violence. Many of the women voiced a preference for incarceration of offenders along with family violence treatment. This preference may have stemmed from a need for validation and safety. These women appeared to equate justice with punishment and rehabilitation. However, it is becoming apparent that incarceration does not always improve chances for rehabilitation or healing. Chapters 4, 5, and 6 discuss some alternative means by which rehabilitation and community re-integration can be accomplished.

Currently, through the *Correction and Conditional Release Act* (Sections 79 to 84), the Aboriginal community has the opportunity to participate with the justice system in amending service provision to better meet the needs of its people. Alternatives such as diversion projects, like the Ganootamaage Justice Services of Winnipeg discussed in Chapter 4, are being suggested and pursued. In some cases, the occasion presents itself for the modification of existing programs to formats that better reflect the Aboriginal experience. Opportunities for new initiatives must be recognized and taken advantage of to maximize the benefits to the Aboriginal community. Funding and resourcing from all levels of government need to be articulated and implemented to make development of policy, legislation and service delivery possible.

This volume presents a number of studies on the effects of colonization, the need for programming specific to and designed by Aboriginal people and the efforts made by the Aboriginal community to meet that need. Chapter 1 presents the current overview of family violence issues in relation to the Aboriginal community. Chapter 2 presents a study conducted by Elizabeth Thomlinson, Nellie Erickson and Mabel Cook that examined community perception of family violence services available in the northern communities of the Swampy Cree Tribal Council, Alberta. Chapter 3 summarizes a study on Aboriginal women's experiences with family violence, their treatment within the criminal justice system, and their views of alternative measures of justice, completed by Anne McGillivray and Brenda Comaskey. In Chapter 4 the Ganootamaage Justice Service of Winnipeg's diversion project is described by Kathy Mallet, Kathy Bent, and Wendy Josephson. This project provides alternative sentencing practices through the use of traditional holistic methods such as healing plans, ceremonies and the involvement of Elders. In Chapter 5 Jocelyn Proulx and Sharon Perrault discuss the work done by the Ma Mawi Wi Chi Itata Family Violence Program both within the community and in Stony Mountain Federal Correctional Facility, in providing a blend of mainstream and Aboriginal-specific programming to help individuals heal from family violence. Chapter 6 of the book is presented by Lawrence Ellerby and colleagues from the Native Clan Organization's Forensic Behavioral Management Clinic. It outlines a program blend of mainstream and Aboriginal-specific approaches to Aboriginal sex offenders.

Communities are encouraged to transpose the information and experiences presented to enhance their provision of services. Post-secondary students will also benefit through having the opportunity to debate and discuss the benefits and pitfalls of Aboriginal-specific programming. It is also anticipated that the publication of this book will encourage individuals from the community and academe to collaborate and work together to solve the issue of family violence.

Chapter 2

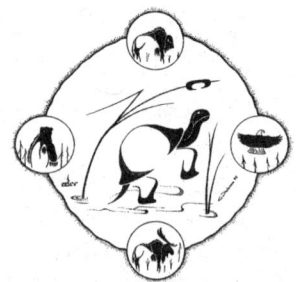

Could This Be Your Community?

Elizabeth Thomlinson, Nellie Erickson and Mabel Cook

Although family violence and violence against women are recognized as widespread social, health and justice problems in all sectors of Canadian society, national epidemiological data are not available to clearly establish the scope of the problem (CPHA, 1994). Comprehensive documentation of the types and frequency of abuse and violence across all ages of the population, at both the provincial and national levels, has not occurred. Based on a national study it is estimated that three out of every ten Canadian women who are, or were, married, experienced physical or sexual abuse by their marital partner (Rodgers, 1994). However, because of the nature of all types of family violence and violence against women, many cases remain unreported while victims continue to suffer in silence. The purpose of this chapter is to describe a research project which was undertaken to, first, determine the resources used by victims of abuse and family violence from seven First Nations communities in northern Manitoba. The second stage of the research sought information on the extent of abuse and family violence from the perspectives of community members. The findings of this study demonstrated an acute awareness of issues surrounding violence and abuse within families and the communities, and the need for reporting and intervention.

The Background
The Aboriginal Justice Inquiry noted that "violence and abuse in Aboriginal communities has reached epidemic proportions" (Hamilton and Sinclair, 1991:481). One report completed for the Royal Commission on Aboriginal Peoples stated that it is impossible to ascertain the extent of family violence in Aboriginal communities,

but nevertheless concluded that family violence within Canada's First Nations is distinctive from that in white communities because "it [violence] has invaded whole communities and cannot be considered a problem of a particular couple or an individual household" (Peoples, 1996:56).

Family violence includes physical, sexual and emotional abuse of women, men and children of all ages. A general population survey in Ontario (MacMillan et al., 1997) revealed that 31 percent of males over fifteen years of age reported a history of childhood physical abuse while 21 percent of females reported being physically abused. More young women (13 percent) reported being sexually abused than did young men (4 percent). These findings were consistent with those previously reported in a national survey in Canada (Badgley, Allard, and McCormick, 1984).

According to national statistics, up to one-quarter of all women have been abused by their current or previous marital partners (CPHA, 1994). However, the Ontario Native Women's Association stressed that family violence is an even greater issue in Aboriginal communities with up to 80 percent of Aboriginal women subjected to abuse and violence (ONWA, 1989). Participants in the ONWA study were also concerned about a lack of social services and culturally appropriate treatment resources to help them deal with the problem.

One widely studied component of family violence is childhood maltreatment, which is an all-inclusive term now used to include physical, sexual and emotional abuse and neglect of children. The long-term effects of childhood maltreatment have been reported to include depression, substance abuse, school problems and lowered self-esteem, as well as self-destructive and aggressive behaviours (Garbarino and Kostelny, 1992; Hall, Sachs, Rayens, and Lutenbacher, 1993). Having a history of childhood maltreatment has also been shown to be a significant predictor of thinking about, planning and attempting suicide (Koniak-Griffin and Lesser, 1996). Studies have also suggested that witnessing violence in the home or community can have a long-term impact on a child's cognitive abilities, school performance and learning (Pynoos and Nader, 1990). In addition, a cyclical pattern may develop within families wherein victims of violence and abuse begin to abuse others, alcohol and drug use escalates, family members neglect themselves and each other, and suicide becomes a means of escape.

In a broad-based effort to address the needs of Aboriginal people, residents of remote and rural communities, members of minority groups and persons with disabilities, the Federal Government provided funding from 1993–1996 for the Family Violence Initiative. Awareness of the problem of family violence and violence against women had been heightened throughout the region where this study was conducted through workshops, seminars and conferences. As well, pamphlets, booklets, posters and videos to address the educational needs of persons of all ages had been made available in all communities.

Initiating the Current Study
In recognizing the significance of the problem of family violence and its impact on their communities, members of the Tribal Council for seven northern Manitoba First Nations decided to instigate actions that would address the needs of the abused and abusers (Thomlinson, Erickson, and Packo, 1996). A resolution was passed by the Tribal Council directing the child and family service agency, and local child care committees, to establish a community approach toward healing for both victims and abusers. A second resolution supported the health centre in the establishment of an inter-agency community to identify funding and programming for prevention and treatment of family violence.

Information about the prevalence of family violence and violence against women in the seven member communities was available through a number of sources such as child and family services, the police, probation services and shelters for victims of violence, located in urban centres. This information could be aggregated with data from the entire regional population. Therefore, members of the health centre decided that a study should be undertaken to compile all available statistics on the extent of family violence in the communities prior to the development of intervention programs.

Reported Cases of Family Violence
The initial stage of the project included gathering information that was a matter of public record from all agencies in northern Manitoba coming in contact with victims and abusers from the seven member communities. No names or confidential information that could identify persons were sought. The agencies included: (a) child and family services, (b) crisis centres and women's shelters, (c) probation services, (d) addiction and treatment centres and services, (e) the courts, (f) police agencies, (g) band-controlled schools and (h) health care institutions and organizations, including nurs-

ing stations. A research assistant, fluent in Cree, was hired from one of the local communities to assist with the project and to liaise with the communities. All agencies were asked to provide their definition of family violence and violence against women, as well as statistics on the numbers of persons served by their agency, where family violence was a factor. The findings from this phase of the study are presented elsewhere (Thomlinson, Erickson, and Cook, 2000); thus they are only briefly summarized below.

The results from this first stage of the research project demonstrated that accurate information on the incidence of family violence/abuse in the region was not available, nor was there a means to compile such data. Services were offered through multiple agencies which meant that there was no clear picture of the magnitude and severity of the problem of violence within the seven member communities. The majority of agencies worked with the victims of violence and/or their abusers in isolation, except in cases of child abuse where there is a provincial government mandate that child-caring agencies and the police work together.

Even though members from a single family may receive services from several different agencies, these agencies did not work together in any collaborative fashion. Each service delivery agency offered their assistance to individual family members with no connection to other experiences affecting the families at that particular time. The inability to obtain a comprehensive picture regarding family violence and violence against women prompted the community members to urge that the second stage of the study proceed with a survey of unreported cases of family violence.

Survey of Unreported Cases

The purpose of this phase of the study was to determine the extent of family violence within the region from the perspective of the community members. Definitions of violence, the impact on individuals and the communities, and suggestions for ways to deal with the problem were sought in order to serve as a basis for future intervention programs.

Method
Procedure
Community members, including local health care employees, assisted in the development of a questionnaire comprised of open-ended questions and checklists. The statistician from the Manitoba

Nursing Research Institute helped the researchers develop and refine the questionnaire. Because English is a second language for many persons in these communities, the survey questions needed to be worded so that they were understandable to all. The questionnaire was tested with other community members to assure the clarity of the questions and the ease of use by the participants.

In each community, the health administrator announced that the study was being conducted. Meetings were also held in the communities, at which time two of the researchers who were fluent in Cree explained the research project. Persons from each community then participated in making the questionnaires available to community members. Self-addressed envelopes were attached to permit the anonymous return of the questionnaires. There were also sealed drop boxes in each community.

Three hundred and fifty questionnaires were distributed within the region, which has a population of 7500 persons. There was an excellent response rate of 75.5 percent or 265 returned questionnaires. Many participants enriched the findings by expanding their answers to include additional information. These comments helped to clarify or, alternatively, raise questions around some of the quantitative information. A deliberate choice was made to aggregate the data from all the communities because the community members believed that their community might be unfairly stigmatized if participants believed there was a significant problem of family violence.

Sample

A purposive sample of persons ten years and older within each community was undertaken with questionnaires distributed to persons in each of six age categories. There were 104 male and 153 female participants (eight persons did not answer this questionnaire). Age distribution of those in the sample is consistent with that of the population which is positively skewed toward the younger age ranges (see Table 2.1). The latest census data for the region show that 58 percent of the population falls within the age range of 10-44 years, with only 7 percent of the population over 55 years of age (Government of Canada, 1996).

Table 2.1

Ages of Persons in the Study Sample						
10–14	15–19	20–24	25–34	35–50	>50	No response
46 (17%)	59 (22%)	30 (11%)	54 (20%)	59 (22%)	10 (4%)	8 (3%)
(discrepancy of 1 percent from rounding)						

Results
Meaning of Family Violence

There was a wide variety of answers to the question "What does family violence/abuse mean to you?" The responses to this question demonstrated an awareness of family violence/abuse in the participants' communities, even if the participants had not experienced violence in their personal lives. As the following sample of responses shows, the efforts of education programs to promote awareness of the problem of violence/abuse are evident.

Violence was identified by some participants as being physical, sexual and emotional abuse, encompassing all ages from children to the elders, including verbal abuse and name calling. One of the most inclusive descriptions of violence was

> *Family violence/abuse means neglecting children, not buying clothing, food, etc. due to excessive gambling, alcohol, drugs. Hitting, fighting, and locking up your spouse. Verbal, physical, mental and spiritual abuse.*

Some participants focused on beatings and physical abuse:

> *Family violence/abuse means when you get hit or beat up by family or friends or anyone;*

> *You get beat up all the time;*

> *Children or wife get hit all the time for no apparent reason.*

Others described the problem of child abuse only: "a parent beating up his or her child physically" and "when a man or woman hits a child."

> *Family violence is a pretty scary situation ... how people are being treated in a bad way*

was one respondent's description of abuse. An adult male noted that abuse occurs

> *when a family member causes another family member pain, suffering, grief through actions.*

Rather than describing what abuse meant to them, a number of participants referred to the frequency of the abuse. Some participants revealed "getting hurt every day." One young man stated "it [family violence] goes on constantly." The depth of the problem was demonstrated in responses such as "when a family member has hurt you in any way that will affect you for the rest of your life." One child in the 10–14 age range stated "I see it all around." Others revealed that abuse should not be concealed; "you should tell someone."

One participant tied abuse to substance addiction:

> *Dysfunctional family, where alcohol is involved, abuse is bound to happen.*

A young person in the 15–19 age range responded with insight into the cycle of violence that may develop by stating that

> *Sometimes my Dad gets mad at my Mom and my Mom will try to not pass it on to me. But it will [be passed on...]*

Another person noted that

> *I still don't fully understand it but I know it's wrong. In order for me to understand I must first accept my own healing.*

One young man revealed his concerns for the problem:

> *Violence happens to my friends and nothing is done again to stop it.*

The responses demonstrated genuine and deep reflection on the question of family violence. The definitions of violence included all types of abuse and neglect and covered all ages of persons. The cycle of violence and the lasting impact of abuse on persons were also illustrated in the responses, demonstrating a high level of awareness amongst the community members.

The Level and Experience of Abuse
Of the 264 persons who responded to the question "Have you ever been abused?" 168 (63 percent) of the participants indicated they had been abused. Of those reporting abuse, 33 (19 percent) had experienced abuse once, 37 (22 percent) had been abused weekly, 10 (6 percent) monthly and 89 (53 percent) once in a while. Two persons added that they were being abused every day, while 10 did not respond to the question. Women were more likely to be abused than were men. Over 70 percent of the women noted they had experienced abuse while 50 percent of the men reported being abused.

A high percentage of participants were aware of family members who had been abused with 202 (76 percent) stating that some, or all, of their family members had experienced violence. The responses ranged from 133 stating family members had been abused once in a while to 25 who said the abuse occurred weekly. One participant had added a comment that family members were being abused on a daily basis. The participants were not asked any questions regarding the relationship of the abused to the abuser. In retrospect, this question would have added valuable information and should be included in any future research on this topic.

One woman described being beaten by her common-law husband with a bottle of liquor. For her the pain of being beaten was ongoing; she cannot forget the abuse. A young man who had been sexually abused continued to have a "bad feeling about himself"; never forgetting or being able to forgive, always remembering and wishing the good times (before the abuse) could come back. These descriptions of abuse provide a vivid picture of the effect of abuse/violence on the victims.

Some participants felt punished and blamed for what had happened to them; they felt ashamed and sorry they had told their stories. One woman noted that now that she knows that the abuse was not her fault, she cannot forgive her parents and others who were involved in what had happened to her.

Reporting the Abuse
While only 98 of the 265 participants responded "yes" to the question "Have you ever reported family violence/abuse?" 131 persons actually checked off that they had reported to a parent, a family member, the RCMP, a priest, a friend and/or various health care and family service professionals. The discrepancy in this response suggests that some participants may have differentiated between reporting to

persons who were seen to be in an official capacity, such as a social worker or the RCMP, and telling a parent, family member or a friend about their abuse. In the development of any future questionnaires the differentiation between reporting to a person in an official capacity and telling another person such as a friend should be clearly made.

The persons who told another person about their abuse noted that they did so to seek help from within, or around, their community to deal with the problem. Just as importantly, 206 participants replied that if they were abused today, they would tell someone about the abuse, while 201 of these participants replied that if they knew of another person who was being abused, they would also tell others. Several persons noted that whether they reported the abuse of others was dependent on what the victim directed them to do, while two others noted that when abuse was happening outside their family it was none of their business.

One man regretted that he did not report his abuse. He is now haunted by the knowledge that a friend was later abused by the same person. Another participant described how her abuse continued until it was reported to the police and the abuser was charged with assault. In some cases, victims of violence noted that they relied on family members to help them rather than contact the police.

Reasons For Not Reporting
Of the participants, 231 knew that family violence/abuse was against the law. However, the fear of going to court would keep 94 of the 265 participants from reporting abuse/violence. As participants noted,

> *Going to court is very scary. The lawyers ask you all these questions and sometimes you don't remember the exact dates when this [the abuse] happened to you. The person who did this [abuse] to you might not even go to jail.*
>
> *Court offers no justice for victims.*
>
> *I was tired of being hurt by the one I love.*
>
> *[They] put it all on me. I swear to God I'll never ask for police help again. I don't trust them. I never will.*

One young mother detailed how she told the police about her

abuse only to have them lay the blame on her. This woman's experience left her believing that she could stop her abuse alone.

One person wrote of the difficulty of getting action from the police when elderly persons are being financially abused by family members. This participant described how she had to address the issues with her siblings because the authorities said they could do nothing. Others noted that nothing happened when they reported the abuse so they now believe that no one cares, they feel alone with nowhere to go, and believe that things will never change; they continue to be abused.

Fear of getting family members into trouble, of breaching confidentiality, that the abuser might come after the one who reported the abuse, that the family might be split up or that parents might lose their children were all cited by participants as reasons why they might not report abuse/violence of which they were aware. Threats from an abuser, not wanting to get involved in another's business and the fact that others in the community might gossip about the victim and the incident would also prevent participants from reporting. One person noted that if she were to report abuse "someone might try and burn my house down. Or someone might try and fight me."

Perceptions of Family Violence in the Community
When asked to indicate what type of violence/abuse they believed to be most prevalent in their community 40 percent of the participants stated that physical, sexual, and emotional abuse were all common, while 31 percent believed physical abuse was the most prevalent, 17 percent said that it was emotional abuse and 11 percent selected sexual abuse as the most common. In response to the question "What type of violence/abuse is the most harmful?" 27 percent of the participants commented that all abuse was harmful, with other responses divided between 39 percent who thought sexual abuse was most harmful, 19 percent who selected emotional abuse, and 15 percent who believed physical abuse to be most harmful to the victim.

While 100 persons believed that sexual abuse was the most painful type of abuse with which to cope, 75 very clearly stated that all abuse was painful, with none being less painful than any other. Many of these participants were distinctly angry that the question "What is the least painful type of abuse to deal with?" had been included in the questionnaire adding many comments such as

> *What a stupid question, they all hurt!*
>
> *They all have the same impact.*
>
> *Everyone hurts in any abuse.*
>
> *All abuse is painful.*
>
> *I can't believe you would have enough nerve to ask a question like this!*

These participants had added the category "all" to the question "What is the most painful type of abuse to deal with?"
    Others who had designated sexual abuse as the most painful abuse noted that

> *it kills the soul forever*

and for a person to

> *heal from sexual abuse they must be emotionally and physically well.*

Reminders of the abuse and bad memories affected other persons:

> *It's in your mind and sometimes something reminds you about that bad memory.*

The Connection to Suicide
Among the study participants there was a strong relationship between the participants' thoughts of, or attempts at, suicide and their personal experience of abuse/violence. One third of those completing the questionnaires responded that they had attempted suicide because of family violence/abuse. Women were more likely to attempt suicide than were men. Of great concern is the fact that 15 of those who have been abused continue to think about committing suicide on a daily basis, while 17 others consider suicide weekly.
    There were two very diverse comments added to this section: one person did not think of suicide, "only Revenge!", while another wrote that he/she thought of suicide "Every Aching Minute."

Some participants described the sadness and helplessness that affects the entire community when a member commits suicide. Others noted how they "felt bad and wished they could help that person." Persons who had thoughts about committing suicide dealt with these thoughts by thinking of their children and how much it would hurt their families and friends if they attempted or actually did commit suicide. Some reminded themselves that, from their perspective, suicide was a coward's way out. Others told themselves that things had to get better, while they thought of the pain that the person who had suicided must have faced.

Services to Intervene in the Community
The majority of participants (186 of 265) responded positively to the question "Are there resources/services within the community where people can go for help to deal with violence/abuse?" There was no identification of what specific services were available in each community. However, 110 of the 265 participants believed that persons seeking help had to go outside the community to receive that help.

When asked "Would you list some things you would like to see that could help people in the community deal with violence/abuse?" participants indicated that a combination of services including youth groups (144), crisis centres (133), healing circles (125) and a regional healing circle (86) would be the most valuable. Youth centres, a wilderness camp, Alcoholic Anonymous and a cultural healing circle were additional services that were added to the surveys. A number of participants added comments that all family members needed to be involved in regular meetings at which they could discuss their problems.

When asked to identify "persons who could help?" youth counsellors (116), the health nurse (65), health administrator (63) and probation officer (50) were most frequently identified as persons who could provide assistance to prevent further violence. In addition, some participants included NADAP (drug and addiction program) counsellors and the involvement of concerned community members who want to help. Elders who understood what victims of violence/abuse were facing, were also identified by several participants as persons to whom they could turn for help.

Participants believed that persons providing services to victims of family violence needed professional education: "nurses meaning...professionals..."; "mental health workers with B.S.Ws

[Bachelor of Social Work]"; and "licensed family violence worker[s]." There were recommendations added to the survey that workers

> *need healing, too, before they can be effective.*

A major concern was that persons working with victims of violence maintain confidentiality. This was often repeated as being essential to gaining trust and being effective.

When asked who should start working on breaking the cycle of family violence, a large proportion (151 participants) placed the responsibility on all of the community members themselves, with 110 adding that the band councils, and 71 that local health boards, needed to be active participants. Of concern was the fact that only 49 persons indicated that the tribal child and family services agency, which has workers in each community, should begin to break the cycle of violence. Caution again was sounded by a number of participants that community leaders and professionals needed to first seek their own healing from violence/abuse before they could be effective role models in the communities. The repetition of this statement suggests that participants do not believe that either the leaders or professionals could be effective unless they recognized the need for, and sought, help for their own experiences with violence/abuse.

The extreme concern felt by some persons was evident in the comments such as

> *Us!!! We'll die off if we don't get help. What good is the future with [messed] up youth?*

This participant emphatically noted that the responsibility to initiate change lay within the community itself. The final comment to which all members of the communities, their leaders and the professionals working within the communities must respond was heavily written in capital letters by a young woman:

> HELP OUR COMMUNITY PLEASE!

Discussion and Recommendations

This survey clearly indicates that the incidence of abuse and violence reported by the participants is high, and that women continue to report being abused in higher proportions than men. Moreover, the proportion of women suffering from abuse/violence is higher than those found by national surveys in Canada. Although the number of women who reported that they experienced violence/abuse (70 percent) is less than the 80 percent reported by the Ontario Native Women's Association (1989), the high numbers in both studies are of major concern.

The meaning of family violence/abuse to participants ranged from neglect of children to drug abuse and physical and sexual violence. Some descriptions emphasized the destructive effects of abuse/violence on the victims. Regardless of the type(s) of family violence/abuse the participants had experienced, the lingering pain has had an effect on the persons involved. Although sexual abuse was considered to be soul-destroying, participants had overwhelmingly emphasized that all types of abuse were painful when they responded to all of the related questions regarding the pain suffered by victims of abuse/violence.

Of grave concern was the high incidence of participants who had attempted suicide, and the relationship between abuse and either attempted or regular thoughts about suicide. This finding is consistent with previous studies which found that completed suicides are higher among males than females (Cooper, Corrado, Karlberg, and Adams, 1992), while suicide attempts are higher among women than men (Strickland, 1997). These findings regarding the number of persons who attempted suicide are consistent with previous studies which indicated that suicide rates among Aboriginal youth are five to six times the national average in Canada and two to three times the average in the United States (Gotowiec and Beiser, 1993, 1994; LaFromboise and Bigfoot, 1988; Strickland, 1997). With no mental health services and only emergency acute care available in each community, the lack of service delivery to persons facing such grave problems could ultimately mean that a relatively large proportion of persons might be successful in their attempts to commit suicide.

Although important, family violence is only one of the multiple factors that have been related to suicide. Having a history of substance abuse, unemployment, poverty and feelings of hopelessness all may be contributing factors to suicide (Cooper et al., 1992; Dexheimer Pharris, Resnick, and Blum, 1997; LaFromboise and Bigfoot, 1988). Interventions to prevent the loss of more lives must take into account the complex interrelationships between all of these factors.

A promising finding of this study is that a large majority of persons noted that if they were currently being abused, or if they knew of someone being abused, they would tell someone. The majority of the participants were aware that family violence/abuse is against the law. An extensive public education program regarding family violence/abuse had been launched in each of the communities from 1993-1996 just prior to, and during, the study. These programs outlined the various types of family violence/abuse and highlighted the laws that should help to protect victims of violence. Nevertheless, the fear of going to court would stop many participants from reporting abuse/violence to the police or child-caring agencies. To have one third of the sample suggest that they feared the court system so much that it would prevent them from reporting to the mandated agencies is a significant problem that must be addressed. If the current system engenders such fear that it is not effective, then there must be consideration of alternative systems generated with the participation of members of the First Nations communities to deal with the problem.

Several factors regarding the availability and use of resources within and outside the community must be considered. Why a substantial number of participants believed that help must be sought from outside the community when they replied that resources were available within the community requires clarification in future research. The authors did hypothesize that the issues that were identified by participants, of lack of trust of local leaders and professionals and a lack of confidentiality within the communities, might be closely tied to seeking help outside rather than within the communities. Participants had emphasized their concerns that professionals and the elected officials in the communities needed to have worked through any personal issues of abuse before they could be effective in helping to lower the level of violence in the communities. This comment was added throughout the survey by numerous participants, who stressed that many in positions of authority could not be trusted. The authors hypothesized that this lack of trust that professionals and leaders had worked through their own issues with violence/abuse would deter victims of violence from seeking help within the communities.

Regional healing centres that use approaches such as healing circles and individual counselling were suggested as primary resources to cope with the problems of family violence and its concomitant effects. There was a call for trained, educated persons to work in the communities. The importance of having professionals who have been educated to take into account, and incorporate, culturally sensitive care as they work with community members to develop local preventative initiatives and interventions cannot be too highly stressed. Core content on the historical and political issues of First Nations, family violence and violence against women, communication skill development and content on ethical and legal issues would provide all professionals with context and skills to practise more effectively in the communities.

Participants frequently repeated that these licensed or professional persons must also have first dealt with their own personal problems before they could successfully intervene with community members. Overwhelmingly participants believed that initiatives and efforts must begin in the local community. Programs from outside the community were not requested.

Further research that builds on this study is essential to address the health and social needs of community members affected by family violence. A study to explore factors affecting the reporting of abuse/violence and relationships with the legal system would provide qualitative data unavailable from a questionnaire. A valuable step would then be to seek support for the development of Aboriginal-specific intervention programs which are community-based to address the needs highlighted by the participants.

Conclusion

Although this study focused on the problems of family violence within seven northern communities and did indeed indicate that family violence/abuse is widespread, these findings must not lead to stereotyping of all families as participating in violence. It must be remembered that many persons had never experienced any family violence. Through education programs on family violence and violence against women over the past six years, community members have developed an awareness of what violence means, the impact on the community and the potential to intervene.

There were no questions in the survey regarding substance use which has been related to both suicide and family violence. Any future studies should incorporate questions on the type, frequency and amount of substance use. The inclusion of socioeconomic factors such as employment, income, housing and other living conditions would also serve to place the issues of violence and suicide within a larger environmental context.

Intervention programs that begin within the community and integrate the wisdom of elders who have sought their own healing were identified by the participants as the most effective means to deal with the multiple issues associated with the violence and abuse. There was the repeated request that professionals working in the communities be well-educated and prepared to work in their roles. Treatment of the whole family, and not just the abused nor the abuser, was recognized as requiring long-term concentrated effort. A healing centre that incorporates traditional teachings and values was requested by many participants as an essential and effective intervention.

This study provided information on the issues of family violence from the perspectives of community members. It may be used as a basis for the development of intervention programs initiated from within each community. The participants demonstrated that the development of programs specific to their communities is essential if the issue of abuse/violence within the communities is to be adequately addressed.

Chapter 3

"Everybody had black eyes"
Intimate Violence, Aboriginal Women and the Justice System
Anne McGillivray and Brenda Comaskey

> *In the reserve just, like, everybody had black eyes walking around, all the ladies, all black. I thought that's the life.... Nobody don't say nothing.*

Introduction
This chapter is a brief summary of a study conducted in the summer of 1995 in partnership with Aboriginal women's service agencies in Winnipeg. Twenty-six Aboriginal women who were assaulted by male partners and had contact with the justice system were interviewed about their experiences of violence and their views on system response. Manitoba's domestic violence policy stresses vigorous criminal prosecution. Alternative approaches to justice are now used in many reserve communities, most geared to sentencing rather than diversion[1] (Green, 1995). An exception is Toronto's Aboriginal Legal Services Diversion Project that gives urban offenders the option of appearing before a peer justice committee in exchange for entering a guilty plea; charges are then stayed. Men charged with partner assault are not accepted by the project. In planning a similar initiative for Winnipeg, the question, "Should Aboriginal men who have assaulted a partner be eligible for diversion?" was raised. This question is the basis of our study.

Despite the immense volume of academic and government reports on Aboriginal peoples in Canada, there remains "a serious lack of research on Aboriginal women" (Canadian Panel, 1993:156). Correlations between abuse in childhood and violent partnerships in adulthood are presumed but the connections have not been closely investigated in this context. Few studies explore the insights and experiences of Aboriginal women close in time to intimate violence, use themes from their insights to construct theory and inform system response, or report with minimal editorial interference. This study was an ideal opportunity to rectify this.

In this chapter, we first outline the Manitoba justice policy and briefly discuss intimate violence with respect to Aboriginal women. We then turn to a description of the study and a synopsis of our findings. No summary can do justice to the richness and complexity of the issues raised by these women. We refer interested readers to the full account of their experiences, set into the context of colonialism, justice system reform and rights, given in our book, *Black Eyes All of the Time: Intimate Violence, Aboriginal Women and the Justice System*.[2]

Manitoba Justice Policy

Nineteenth-century feminism brought wife battering into the public forum. With the second wave of feminism in the 1960s and 1970s, campaigns to recognize domestic assault as crime intensified, challenging the invisibility of wife battering and the dominant view that intimate violence was rare, confined to the lower-income families, and "consensual"—a view compounded by police, prosecutorial and judicial misreading of victim ambivalence. Police refused to lay charges unless the victim pursued her complaint and prosecutors routinely dropped cases despite significant evidence of serious assault (McGillivray, 1987). Justice response to assault in a domestic context was markedly different from "stranger" and public violence.

Provinces adopted "no-drop" charge and prosecution policies in the early 1980s to correct this disparity in treatment. The 1983 Manitoba directive required that charges be laid in all complaints, and that cases be prosecuted vigorously. Gaps remained in policing, prosecution and bail, while the inadequacies of protection orders were a "common denominator" in all cases (Pedlar, 1991). That such orders were "just a piece of paper" exemplified the gap between "law-as-legislation" and "law-as-practice" (Smart, 1989). In 1990, the directive was reinforced with a "zero-tolerance" policy and the Manitoba Family Violence Court began operation. The first court in North America to deal exclusively with intimate violence cases from charge to disposition, it was to be sensitive to the dynamics of intimate violence, facilitate victim services, expedite cases and relieve case backlog (Ursel, 1991).

In 1993, the *Criminal Code* was amended to accommodate "stalking" or criminal harassment. Also in 1993, Winnipeg Police Services introduced protocols for domestic violence response. An unintended consequence of these developments was a steep increase in unfounded charges against women complainants, necessitating a "counter-accusation charging directive" (directive used to determine if counter charges represent actual abuse of self-defence behaviours) in 1994. A computer database for protection orders was established but access was limited to certain police forces. The measures did not resolve existing problems with the system response (Coalition, 1995; NDP Caucus Task Force, 1995; Prairie Research Associates, 1994). An inquiry into the murder-suicide of an estranged couple—the Lavoie Inquiry—was called in 1996 to review failures in system response (Schulman, 1997). A police officer testifying at the hearings described "modest shortcomings" in domestic violence response—failure to follow protocol, "bargaining out" stalking charges, incomplete computer information, too few special police, poor follow-up and failure to flag records with a history of intimate violence.[3]

Intimate Violence and Aboriginal Women

Normalization of intimate violence in isolated Aboriginal communities is a major barrier to protecting women and children. Community denial of the violence, or its definition as natural, cultural or inevitable hinders victims from defining it as a problem that can be helped, and complicates system response (McGillivray, 1987). If violence by a person in a position of intimate trust, such as a parent or partner, is perceived as the norm, then escaping from the violence means abandoning everyday life. Aboriginal women in Canada experience consistently higher rates of reported intimate violence than the overall female population. At least one in three is abused by a partner, compared with one in ten women overall (Thompson Crisis Centre, 1988), and some estimates are as high as nine in ten (McGillivray, 1987). Four in five have witnessed or experienced intimate violence in childhood (Kiyoshk, 1990; Ontario Native Women's Association, 1989). As bleak as they are, these statistics do not reflect the subjective experience of abuse or the experience of community and justice system responses to violence.

Intimate violence is culturally constructed. Linkages between "race" and meanings assigned to violence occurring within that context are complex. Differences in meaning have an impact on policing, prosecution and access to social services. Thus the dynamics of intimate violence as a public concern may differ in significant ways for many Aboriginal women. Ambiguities in assessing one's own condition as "battered," "abused" or "beaten" (McGillivray, 1987) are compounded where violence has become normalized in a closed or isolated community. Physical and cultural distance from policing, child protection and victim services complicate identification and response. These deficiencies may be further compounded by band politics and band council powers of banishment where, in some cases, victims and social services staff have been banned from their reserves.

The study of Aboriginal peoples in Canada increased significantly in the 1990s. Public inquiries such as the 1996 Royal Commission on Aboriginal Peoples (RCAP) and the 1991 Manitoba Aboriginal Justice Inquiry (AJI) investigated the justice system's impact on Aboriginal peoples within the wider context of colonialism and culture. These and other reports and studies are almost unanimous in finding that Aboriginal people are vastly over-represented in the criminal justice system, many Aboriginal communities are troubled by high rates of all forms of violence including wife battering and child abuse; and alternative justice measures based on traditional Aboriginal cultural values of healing, restitution and reintegration are desirable. These include diversion (not laying charges or dropping charges in order to divert an offender to a program outside the criminal justice system), alternative sentencing measures such as healing circles and First Nations administration of justice. Aboriginal dispute resolution is reintegrative and community-based (Green, 1995), concerned with "atonement to the individual who was wronged" rather than with deterrence and punishment (Canadian Panel, 1993:167). However, experiences of culture and cultural colonization are not uniform. It cannot be assumed that Aboriginal women subjected to intimate violence will view such "cultural" solutions in the same way as their male perpetrators, researchers, political leaders or, perhaps, women more distanced from past experiences of violence. As this present study demonstrates, alternative justice measures are problematic when seen from the perspective of Aboriginal women who have more recently experienced partner violence.

As noted above, Manitoba domestic assault policy stresses vigorous prosecution of violent partners, but the over-representation of

Aboriginal offenders in the criminal justice system is a major concern (Manitoba, 1991; Royal Commission, 1993, 1996; Canadian Bar Association, 1989).[4] The silence that surrounded the brutal rape and murder of a young Aboriginal woman, Helen Betty Osborne, by a gang of non-Aboriginal men has come to symbolize the inadequacies of mainstream responses to violence against Aboriginal women. Yet the cultural disorientation, lack of rehabilitation and anger accompanying penal experiences for Aboriginal offenders may itself escalate violence against partners and others.

Violence against women was not introduced by Euro-colonial contact, nor did matriarchal and matrilineal cultures necessarily preclude it. Emma LaRocque (1996:14) writes:

> We know enough about human history that we cannot assume that all Aboriginal traditions universally respected and honoured women.... It should not be assumed, even in those original societies that were structured along matrilineal lines, that matriarchies necessarily prevented men from oppressing women. There are indications of male violence and sexism in some Aboriginal societies prior to European contact and certainly after contact.

As Patricia Monture-Okanee states, a notable difference is that "aboriginal women do not share with Canadian women the history of *legally sanctioned* violence against women" (1992:256, emphasis added). Cultural and economic destruction of Aboriginal societies, cultural devaluation, sexual abuse and corporal punishment in residential schools, and forced reculturation of children through schooling and child welfare intervention are factors central to the explanations of current rates of Aboriginal violence. One remedy is the restoration of Aboriginal cultural processes. However, our study found that women abused by partners valued the symbolic role of punishment and the practical value of incarceration above cultural or neo-traditional approaches to justice.

The Study
In order to answer the question of whether provincial domestic violence policy should prevail in diversion programs for Aboriginal offenders, the views of Aboriginal women subjected to partner violence are central. A committee of Aboriginal women's service providers and a university researcher was formed, a bibliography

was prepared and a qualitative study using a two-stage, open-ended interview method was designed. Aboriginal women were trained as interviewers and twenty-six women chosen from the files of four local agencies[5] serving Aboriginal women were interviewed. Provisions were made to protect participants emotionally and physically, and to ensure confidentiality. Participants were to have undergone several counselling stages as a criterion of participation. Signed consent forms were administered by service providers. Participants chose their own interview locations and were given a list of social service agencies at the end of the interview. The data were separated so that participants could not be identified by their responses.

Part I of the study investigated participants' background, experiences of violence in childhood and as partners, and the support, intervention and services they received. Part II investigated their views on the purpose of the justice system and their experiences with it, as victims and, in some cases, as offenders. This set the stage for questions on their opinion of alternative justice measures in intimate violence cases. In view of recent changes in prosecutorial policy, participants who experienced intimate violence within five years of the study were included so that their responses could be analyzed within the context of current Manitoba justice policy.

The Participants
The twenty-six women in this study ranged in age from twenty-one to fifty-one years. Education levels ranged from Grade Seven to university completion. Annual income was distributed as follows: under $10,000 (69 percent); $10,000 to $20,000 (23 percent); and over $20,000 (8 percent) for a total of twenty-six participants.[6] Twenty-three were Status Indians (a legal designation with accompanying benefits and restrictions) and three were non-Status Indian or Métis. All but one woman had children. Fourteen had children living apart from them and one woman with legal custody of her child was banned from her reserve, where the child lived with her abusive partner.

Experiences of Violence
The normalization of violence impeded self-awareness and seeking help. The women struggled with self-definition of violence and complaints were disbelieved due to community denial. The following comments exemplify this situation:

> *I thought it was normal to be hit ...to hit or be hit.*
>
> *I tried to get help from my family ... they laughed at me. Of course, each and every one of us grew up in a violent home. I guess they thought it was normal.*
>
> *I didn't know I needed help. I thought it was normal.*
>
> *I didn't think anybody would believe me.*
>
> *I never asked, because I thought no one would understand.*

Participants had as many as five abusive partners. All but one witnessed intimate violence during childhood. All but two (or 92 percent) experienced severe childhood abuse ranging from sexual assault (65 percent) to physical assault (73 percent) and emotional abuse or neglect (42 percent). Violence in childhood was part of everyday life, as the following comments illustrate:

> *Well, when I was five, my dad tried to kill my mom. I was raped by my brother at fifteen and mom died when I was fourteen.*
>
> *My mom and step dad would sometimes physically abuse me, but then my uncles and cousins would sexually abuse me, or people from parties and stuff.*
>
> *It was very lonely ... a lot of neglect and sexual abuse—and physical—no stability, very dysfunctional family.*
>
> *My older sister knew and all she did—I was made to feel so bad—I told the priest I had sex [but I had been raped]. It was really sad. I didn't realize back then that I was a victim. I don't know, making a child feel so bad.*
>
> *If I could take Child and Family Services to court for the abuse that I suffered because of the homes that they put me in, I'd win.*

The line between child and adult abuse was blurred for nine women, who had violent partners in adolescence:

> *I was fifteen.... I didn't realize it was an abusive relationship*

> *because I was young, and I didn't understand what was happening to me.*
>
> *Probably when I was thirteen.... My stepmother, she kicked my father out of the house so we had nowhere to stay in the city ... so I ended up staying with this guy I was seeing, and that is how I got involved in drinking and that, and that is how the abuse started.*
>
> *Even when I stayed with him when I was fifteen.... All night he'd talk about my old boyfriends.... What he did, he tried to hurt me down there.... When I was about four months pregnant, he gave me VD [sexually transmitted infection]. In my second pregnancy, he gave me another VD. And he would cry, cry, "I'm sorry, it'll never happen again."*

Childhood experiences of violence merged into violent teenage relationships. Violence became a hallmark of adult relationships:

> *He beat me three to four times a day. I constantly had black eyes, thick lips, bruises to the body, dislocated shoulder ... always ripping my hair out. He never let me out of his sight.*
>
> *It started off very slow, like a slap here or a slap there, name calling. From then on, I should have got out, but I didn't realize at the time, you know? I was trying to change him to somebody he was not.... It started getting worse and worse.... He knew I would always take him back.... I try not to remember, I don't want to remember, I guess.*
>
> *It was years he was hitting me but ... for me the hardest part was the name calling. He would call me down in my own language [Ojibwa]. He would just sit me down on the bed and call me down for hours without stopping. He would only stop to take a shot of beer or something. He could go for three or four hours.*

These women experienced physical, sexual, emotional, verbal and financial abuse. They were raped, punched, beaten and choked. They were assaulted with guns and knives as well as objects such as tables, blocks of wood and even a metal milk churn. They were humiliated and forcibly detained. Their lives and the lives of their children were threatened.

Coping with Violence
The women coped with the violence in a variety of ways: involving social workers or neighbours, joking about the violence and slashing one's arms to relieve tension.

> *I just asked when I was fourteen years old, I asked to be put in a foster home.*

> *I asked my neighbour if she would call the police if I banged on the wall three times. I lived in a row house so ... I would bang on the wall and she would call if I was not able to do it myself.*

> *My friends would say, "It's time to get up and go home for your daily beating." We began joking about things like that.*

> *I used to see my dad and common-law always fighting when they would drink. That is where I got slashing of arms—from my dad's wife. She used to do that.*

The women struggled with seeing the violence in their lives as a problem and complaints were disbelieved due to community denial or the abuser's social status within the community:

> *On the reserve, all they do is talk about couples, like, those workers there ... they do want married couples to stay together, no matter what ... they don't care how much—they don't care if—there is an abuse there. They take the woman out of the house for a while and ... put them back to the spouse.*

> *Nobody wanted to be involved. They knew how crazy [name of abuser] was, he was capable of anything ... we have a CFS [child and family services] agency and they won't even touch him because they know him. He knows the policies and stuff like that. He knows his way around. He's very knowledgeable ... very good with his mouth.*

> *He was a medicine man [and] many people felt they couldn't assist me, because of my husband's position. Many thought I was lying.*

Police Response
Fear was a frequent reason for staying in an abusive relationship—fear of accelerating the violence, being alone, leaving children behind

or having children apprehended. Fear deterred calling police—fear of not being believed, of victim-blaming and racism, of police simply not showing up. But inadequacy of services on-reserve meant that police were often the only source of help.

> *I didn't want to call the police because I was scared of what this person was capable of, because of his threats to kill or his threats to commit suicide right in front of the kids.*
>
> *He threatened me a lot of times. He told me that the cops were his friends, and he would easily get information from the cops where I was and where I would be.*
>
> *I was terrified that he might be worse than before.*
>
> *I didn't want the police there. I was most scared they would take my kids away.*
>
> *I didn't want him to go to jail.*
>
> *Also the threat of him telling me he was going to leave me.... I didn't want to be alone.*

Fears of racism and victim-blaming by police officers were borne out:

> *I was starting to not want to call them, because, I don't know, they made me feel like somehow it's my fault.*
>
> *There were a lot of times when I did call.... I don't think they believed me. Or else they would take one look at me and say, well, I got a lot of smart comments from them, like, "You probably deserved it, look how drunk you are. If I had an old lady like you that was as mouthy, I would slap her around, too, you know."*
>
> *My head had bumps all over it and my forehead too. My chin was bruised. And they asked me to press charges, those native cops, and I said no and I told them I didn't want any trouble.... He didn't get charged.... Maybe if the RCMP was there. You know how it is on the reserve.*
>
> *The staff sergeant was upset with me, he says, "I'm getting pretty*

> upset with you. You're always phoning, calling here, you're getting to be a bloody nuisance.... I should charge you for harassing, phoning here all the time."

> *Because they always seemed like they were getting disgusted with you, because it is repeated over and over again, being abused and then charge him, and then it would happen again, being abused and then I would charge him. Pretty soon it seemed like even the police or whoever got tired of it and didn't take it seriously any more.*

> *I called the police quite a few times, I'd say about ten times in total in the four years I was with this person. That's including the times when I would call them and they wouldn't show up because they probably looked on their computer and said "Oh, it's her again" ... there were times he would make me phone them back and say we didn't need them to come.*

Fear also impelled decisions to leave:

> *I knew if I stayed in the relationship I'd be dead. So I had to figure out a way to leave.*

Justice System Response

Despite zero tolerance policies, charges were laid in only nineteen of the many hundreds of incidents described by the women (many incidents were not reported, and in some cases, charges were not laid following a report). In five of these cases, charges were dropped—a ratio of one in four. One woman changed her mind. Three women were coerced into dropping charges by the abuser. In one case, the band council requested that charges be dropped. Counter-charges (charges laid against the complainant) were laid against three complainants:

> *I was charged under the zero-tolerance policy. My ex-husband counter-charged me.... [Charges] were dropped because I had a witness that was there at the time and denied I ever hit him.*

> *You both get charged even if you're defending yourself, apparently. It's not fair if you're defending yourself.*

Protection orders were almost impossible to enforce:

> *You have to have this restraining order with you twenty-four hours a day for it to work. I did not know that. They can easily be torn up, your partner can just take it, grab it, and rip it, and it's your word against theirs.*

> *He kind of took the paper and ripped it up.*

> *[I] got a non-molestation order against him. He violated the order seven times. And I'm still waiting for my restraining order to come through.*

> *Even though I know I have the law backing me up it is still me that has to do the calling and deciding, and none of my partners have respected or obeyed these restraining orders.*

> *I've got a restraining order right now.... I called 911 because he was smashing out my car windows, and that was about two weeks ago. I still have not talked to the police on that 911 call.*

> *He stayed in the vehicle so he couldn't breach his order ... taunting me. And because he used to be a police officer himself, he knew the ins and outs of the system.*

Experiences of the judicial process varied. Some of the women were pleased with the help they received but others were faced with inadequate support programs, delays, confusion and intimidation. As these women said:

> *It takes too long ... the woman loses sight of why she brought her old man to court ... he would sweet talk to me.... "Would you drop the charges?". ... He had his chance to work on me.*

> *They seem to be dragging it out for too long [ten months].... That's too long, I think.*

> *The way the judge sits higher up than anyone else and people are sitting on opposite sides of the room—it's just set up like a battle zone.*

> *It was hard to be a witness ... against someone that you live with, because you are so used to being blamed for everything, that you can*

> sit in court knowing it is not your fault, [but] you still feel like it is.

Experiences with lawyers—family lawyers, crown attorneys and defence counsel for women facing counter-charges—were similarly varied:

> The lawyer that I have, I've known him on a personal level, he guided me through the whole process and I feel confident with him because he specializes in abuse cases.

> Well, my lawyer is a woman ... she helped me a lot, like my good friend. She helped me with my phone bill, and my non-molestation order. And I won child custody, but back on the reserve it's hard to get my kids.

> Right away the lawyer will say, "How many times did you get a beating?" When you say, "I didn't," they kind of look at you, like, what are you doing here? They don't realize the emotional or mental [abuse] is just as bad ... the crown are not trained properly to defend the victims.

> I wish that more lawyers would have a better understanding and compassion for the victims.... Lawyers are supposed to be there to help you, not to make you feel worse.

If court is difficult and lawyers variable, is diversion preferable?

Jail or Diversion?
Jail was seen as providing both punishment and safety. Jail means punishment and punishment means recognition by the offender and the community of the harm done. All of the women felt that sentencing is far too lenient. The symbolic function of jail as denunciation and "pay-back," or retribution, was important to all participants. Equally important was the "time-out" for victims when the offender was safely put away:

> He had to see what he was doing was wrong, that it was a criminal act ... it hurts me when I see a person like that [in jail] but he has to learn for what he done wrong.

> When he went to jail I was no longer scared or afraid because I knew

> where he was and he couldn't do any harm to me, at least for a while.
>
> For me, when my abuser was in jail, I felt safe. I'm sure I'm not the only one that feels like that.

Yet sentencing was widely viewed as inadequate. Twenty-three of the women wanted direct input into sentencing:

> I would love to see the judges listen to the victims and really understand where the victim is coming from to the point where they ask the victim what they feel would be a fair sentence and take that into consideration ... the abuser is getting away with a slap on the wrist and the victim is right back where they started from.
>
> Providing them with a woman's point of view of being abused.
>
> I would like to see only one change ... that I would appear in court so they could hear my side of the story, my version, but instead he just pleaded guilty.

Jail alone is not the optimal solution. Treatment combined with a jail term (or a lock-up treatment centre, as suggested by one woman) were seen as most effective in the long term:

> A person can go to jail and just do their time and walk out, and with the same intention they will repeat. I would feel that they would have to go through some rehabilitation program, anger management.
>
> I don't know if Manitoba has a treatment centre for prisoners. They should build one, try to get one anyways. It gets the prisoners to better understand themselves, where they come from, why they abuse, why they commit crimes and all of that.

Despite pressure to move away from the justice system towards First Nations community-based alternatives, participants would not accept diversion and alternative sentencing unless it does what jail is now seen as doing, however unsuccessfully: punish, actually and symbolically; and protect, at least long enough so that victims can get their lives back on track. Participants want input into sentencing, longer sentencing, effective protection order enforcement and effective and mandatory abuser treatment.

Reflections

In these views is a picture of a justice system still struggling with the "new" crimes of intimate violence. The picture shows, as well, a justice system in conflict with race—as culture, as difference, as meaning—and in conflict with its own racism in policing, legal services and bail and sentencing courts. The twenty-six women in this study collectively experienced thousands of incidents of physical, sexual and emotional violence in childhood and adulthood, inflicted by well over a hundred perpetrators—*"the whole damn community,"* as one said. Yet few incidents came to the attention of social service agencies, shelters or the justice system. Women were initiated into intimate violence in childhood through witnessing and experiencing it in every form. Childhood set the stage for their adult lives. This reflects the interconnectedness of intimate violence across the life span and points to the importance of examining childhood in the study of violence in intimate adult relationships.

The high rate of violence may not be unusual for women in shelters or transition homes, from which more than half our sample was drawn, or for women who have approached treatment programs, who form the remainder. It does reflect astounding rates, frequency and severity of intimate violence and lends support to studies that point to the heightened risk of abuse for Aboriginal women. Almost all participants experienced intimate violence while living on reserve. Emotional abuse—public and private rituals of humiliation, spiritual abuse, threats, stalking—was the most damaging and least publicly recognized form of abuse, eroding participants' capacity for independent thought and action.

Lack of services on reserve and reserve politics complicated getting help and getting out. Leaving was less a response to a single incident than the culmination of numerous incidents of violence, tiredness, anger, concern for children and fear of being killed. The women praised the agencies that referred them to the study, but strongly criticized many other services. Shelters and police and agency services for reserve communities range from inadequate to non-existent. Winnipeg services are not adequate even for city residents, yet they serve most of Manitoba. While men leave reserves in search of economic opportunities, women leave because of abuse (LaRocque, 1993). Urban resources will remain a necessity for many Aboriginal women but most important is the improvement of conditions for women and children in their home communities. Leaving one's community means leaving social supports such as family and friends, and sometimes one's own children. The AJI (Manitoba, 1991) took the position that women should never have to leave their reserves because of violence. Without safety, support and healing structures, and without strong community commitment to ending the violence, women and children will continue to be driven away.

In the meantime, for the women in this study, the criminal justice system remains the dominant and external voice in discourses of abuse. They valued its symbolic function and saw it as the ultimate arbiter of violence and its meaning, beyond the control of a sweet-talking abuser or a community in denial. Its purpose, as they saw it, is to punish violence, protect the vulnerable and provide a time of safety by keeping dangerous people in jail. Yet it often failed them. Jail terms were not given often enough or for long enough periods to warn or punish abusers or give victims an adequate period of safety. Yet they did not prefer alternative resolutions, nor did they reject the system on cultural grounds. Treatment would be a *"good thing"* if it can be made to work, but *"time-out"* for self-reconstruction and self-treatment was of more immediate importance. While jail alone does not reform offenders, treatment alone was seen as manipulable—*"an easy way out"*—and was an inadequate response to their suffering and their needs.

Community-based dispute resolution was, in the women's eyes, partisan and subject to political manipulation. They would accept diversion only if it guards against manipulation, takes into account the seriousness of the offence, punishes in some way, gives victims safety, respects disclosures of abuse by offenders as well as victims, offers treatment and monitors compliance.[7] In fact, such holistic responses to intimate violence do exist. They are the result of grass-roots movements around the world that bring together victims, local communities, and justice and social services personnel. The Duluth, Minnesota Domestic Abuse Intervention Project has become a model for coordinated inter-agency and justice system action in response to domestic violence, by combining victim safety and choice with offender treatment and punishment under a complex of closely-monitored protocols. The model has proven successful in both urban and rural settings. It has been adapted by, and for, mixed and indigenous communities such as Saskatoon, Saskatchewan; Hilo, Hawaii; and Hollow Water, Manitoba (Turner, 1995; Merry, 1997; Hollow Water, 1993). These projects ensure that the victim has a strong voice, independent advocacy and support and continued control over her situation, and that the court, circle or other tribunal is thoroughly educated in the dynamics of abuse. This makes it possible to divert selected offenders (or all offenders, as in the Hollow Water goal) from the criminal justice system. The collective experience gained in the course of these projects gives legitimacy to diversion and to the design of other alternative measures.

Childhood violence, isolation and racism shaped and controlled the ability of participants to define their situation as abuse and get help. "Being Native" touched almost every aspect of their experiences of policing, social services and the justice system. Many were silenced by failures in service provision, the normalization of violence within their communities and kinship networks and band politics supporting the abuser. Victim isolation caused by the geography and culture of reserve settings and urban ghettos is worsened by the elaborate strategies of isolation imposed on them by abusers, including: shaming, humiliation and spirit murder; threats against them and their children; physical incapacitation; economic control; public harassment; and blaming them for their own abuse. Many internalized this blame and held themselves responsible for their injuries. They were given little or no assurance of support and protection during the relationship or the extremely dangerous process of "getting out."

If normalization of intimate violence in isolated Aboriginal communities accounts in part for its high risk for Aboriginal women and children, then cultural solutions will not be seen as important. Alternative measures were viewed by the women as being much too easily controlled by abusers and their supporters. The justice system remains central in redefining abuse as a crime and stopping it, despite the fact that it is hard to get there and its protection is often severely compromised. The development of holistic community-driven approaches to the problem holds promise for reserves as well as for urban centres like Winnipeg. Such approaches initially involve the justice system but may lead to alternative systems that satisfy the goals identified by the women in this study: a strong voice in the process, protection and healing for themselves and their children, and accountability and healing for offenders.

Notes

1. Where diversion measures move cases away from the criminal justice system at the charging stage (e.g., a guilty plea is entered, charges are dropped and the case is dealt with outside the system), alternative sentencing measures (e.g., community sentencing circles) would be

applied to cases after conviction in the criminal justice system.
2. A complete account and analysis is available in Anne McGillivray and Brenda Comaskey, *Black Eyes All of the Time: Intimate Violence, Aboriginal Women and the Justice System*, University of Toronto Press, 1999. The 1995 Winnipeg study on which these works are based would not have come into being without the support of the Elizabeth Fry Society, Ikwe-Widdjiitiwin, Ma Mawi Wi Chi Itata Centre Family Violence Program, Native Women's Transition Centre, and Original Women's Network. Research was funded by Heritage Canada and the Seventh Generation Fund and sponsored by the Manitoba Research Centre on Family Violence and Violence Against Women (now RESOLVE). Ethical approval was granted by the Ethics Committee of the Faculty of Law, University of Manitoba. Our work is dedicated to the twenty-six women who shared their experiences with us in the hope that things will change and others will be helped. A version of this chapter was published as: McGillivray, Anne, and Brenda Comaskey. 1998. "'Everybody had black eyes ... nobody don't say nothing': Intimate Violence, Aboriginal Women, and Justice System Response," in Kevin Bonnycastle and George Rigakos, (eds.), *Unsettling Truths: Battered Women, Policy, Politics, and Contemporary Research in Canada*. Vancouver: Collective Press. This version appears with the permission of Collective Press.
3. The Lavoie Inquiry Implementation Committee has acted on the recommendations from the Schulman Report (Ursel, 1998). Responses to the recommendations include: three supervised access centres (Winnipeg, Brandon and Thompson); expanded counselling services in Brandon and Winnipeg; six additional Crown attorneys for the Family Violence Unit; the establishment of a Family Violence Unit Information Line; domestic violence Crown attorneys and Women's Advocacy workers in Bail Court; increased staff for the Women's Advocacy Program; expansion of the Victims First Cellular Phone Program; introduction of The Domestic Violence and Stalking Prevention, Protection and Compensation Act; and stronger responses to offenders including bail briefs, videotaping victim statements, more probation officers, and new technology to control phone calls from correctional institutions.
4. About three percent of the population of Canada is of First Nations origin. Nineteen percent of all admissions to carceral institutions (and up to 90 percent in some institutions) are Aboriginal men. Rates are even higher for Aboriginal women, who account for 50 percent of women incarcerated in provincial institutions and 20 percent in federal institutions (Statistics Canada, 1991).
5. Participants were chosen from the following agencies: Ma Mawi Wi Chi Itata Centre, which provides counselling services to women, children and men; Native Women's Transition Centre, a second-stage housing project; Ikwe-Widdjiitiwin, a short-term crisis shelter; and Elizabeth Fry Society, which provides resources and support to women who are at risk of, or have come into conflict with, the law.

6. The number of women dropped to twenty-five for the second interview because one woman decided not to continue with the study due to personal problems.
7. Winnipeg's Ganootamaage Justice Services does not accept men charged with crimes of violence against partners. At present, no exceptions based on culture are made to Manitoba's zero-tolerance policy.

Chapter 4

Aboriginal Ganootamaage Justice Services of Winnipeg (AGJSW)[1]

Kathy Mallett, Kathy Bent and Dr. Wendy Josephson

Introduction

It has been recognized that the mainstream justice system in Canada has been ineffective in dealing with Aboriginal offenders (LaPrairie, 1996 and 1994; Bonta, LaPrairie, and Wallace, 1997; Bonta, Lipinski, and Martin, 1993; Lee, 1992; York, 1990). Aboriginal people have been overrepresented in the penal system for many years (Canadian Justice Statistics, 1994). Nearly 50 percent of all admissions into the Manitoba penal system are people of Aboriginal descent (Native Affairs Secretariat, 1998). Reports of discriminatory practices towards Aboriginals have been emerging at alarming rates. Discriminatory practices are related to all aspects of the justice system including policing, courts, and correctional services. Most of these discriminations are reported to be systemic in nature (for example, a refusal to plea bargain because it contradicts the basic cultural tenet of telling the truth and therefore being disadvantaged in sentencing), although many could be termed as overt discriminatory acts (for example, verbal and physical assault) (Manitoba 1991). Systemic discrimination, most often pertaining to language and cultural barriers, arises because of inadequately informed justice staff. Nonetheless, it is evident that these disparities have caused a great turmoil in the Aboriginal and non-Aboriginal communities, and have also created an enormous financial burden (for example, the general legal and incarceration costs) for Canadian society. Therefore, much effort on the part of Aboriginal communities and the mainstream justice system in Canada has been initiated to address some of the issues pertaining to discrimination and other problems contributing to the overrepresentation of Aboriginal people in the criminal justice system.

In Manitoba, the efforts of Aboriginal community leaders, members of the non-Aboriginal community and officials from the mainstream justice system to investigate this problem resulted in the formation of the Aboriginal Justice Inquiry of Manitoba (AJI). Its report (Manitoba, 1991) reiterated the discriminatory practices that Aboriginals face in almost all areas of the justice system. The report also encouraged optimism in the Aboriginal community because it put forth recommendations to address some of these issues.

One of these issues involved the sentencing component of the current judicial process. Sentencing is the final step in the process and sometimes involves incarceration. This form of sanction is known to be the most expensive and least effective, in terms of cost, for the justice system and for Aboriginal families. Aside from excessive financial strain on the criminal justice system, personal costs are incurred when Aboriginal families are separated as a result of incarceration. In this context, the AJI recommended that

> What is needed is a philosophy of sentencing that would make less use of correctional facilities, strengthen the use of community sanctions, address the needs of victims and offenders, give proper consideration to cultural factors when formulating sentences and allow the community to play a meaningful role in the development and monitoring of sentences. (1991:390)

This recommendation was instrumental in the development of a program offering alternative sentencing practices for Aboriginals in Manitoba—Aboriginal Ganootamaage Justice Services of Winnipeg (AGJSW). This program is the first of its kind in Manitoba and was modelled after a similar program in Toronto.

This chapter will examine the development of this program, describing the manner in which it has worked to avoid or minimize incarceration, foster Aboriginal values of reconciliation with victims (as opposed to the retributive measures of mainstream justice systems) and involve the Aboriginal traditional community through the participation of Elders and the use of traditional healing methods. The success of this essentially holistic approach to offender treatment will be evaluated.

History of Aboriginal Ganootamaage Justice Services of Winnipeg

In 1994 CBC radio aired a report on an innovative Aboriginal criminal justice diversion program operating in Toronto entitled "Aboriginal Legal Services of Toronto" (Community Council Project, 1992). This report aroused interest and in the Winnipeg community where it was felt that this type of program would be ideal (MNAS, 1999). A steering committee consisting of Aboriginal and non-Aboriginal community members was formed in order to discuss the concept. The committee included distinguished members of the legal and justice system, health and social services groups and the general business sector. Fagie Fainman, a retired criminal defense lawyer and consultant of the Original Women's Network, was retained by the committee. She investigated the Aboriginal Legal Services of Toronto program for the steering committee, who then developed a conception paper, incorporating recommendations from the AJI and the Toronto program.

The conception paper was presented to Aboriginal organizations in the city of Winnipeg and members of the Aboriginal community at large in order to solicit ideas and recommendations. The most positive feedback came from a group of Elders from the Manitoba Association for Native Languages (MANL) who offered their resounding support. Eventually, the concept was deemed viable and the development of a proposal ensued.

The proposal put forth the concept of a coordinated centralized legal system with three components: 1) The Court Workers Program, 2) Aboriginal Community Council Diversion Program and 3) Legal Aid Clinic. The Court Workers, Program and the Legal Aid Clinic serve as support units to the Community Council Diversion Program. The Court Workers Program is the link between the Council and the Manitoba justice system. It has been in existence for a number of years. The Aboriginal Legal Aid Clinic has been operational since 1996. However, the exact nature of the relationship between these two programs and the new Diversion program is still evolving.

Central to the proposal was the diversion process, which is based on a combination of principles derived from restorative justice models. The models include the Community Council Forum, Community

Justice Forum and Sentencing Circles. This program format provides a forum to foster reconciliation, restitution and restoration of peace and harmony for the Aboriginal offender and the victim. The central principles arise from an Aboriginal value system and cultural beliefs. An emphasis is placed on holistic and spiritual healing, integration with immediate and extended family, community participation in the development of a healing plan and the collective determination of appropriate reparations. Once the Aboriginal offender voluntarily agrees to participate and completes a healing plan, charges, if any, are stayed by the Crown Attorney. Consequently, in a manner similar to the conditional and absolute discharges in the mainstream justice system, a court appearance is not required and no charges are entered in the criminal record.

The diversion process is designed to represent and support the Aboriginal offender utilizing Aboriginal traditions. Hence, Ganootamaage, meaning "speaking for" in the Ojibway language, was adopted as the name for the program. It took a number of years before the proposal was approved by its main funders, the governments of Manitoba and Canada. AGJSW then opened an office in January of 1998 and began setting up structures for implementing the diversion program. In this chapter the diversion process is thoroughly described beginning with an overview of the staff composition.

Aboriginal Ganootamaage Justice Services of Winnipeg Staff
The Board of Directors
A Board of Directors representing the community as a whole is the primary governing body of AGJSW. The board consists of members of the Aboriginal and non-Aboriginal community who have expertise in many areas. Members include a police officer with the City of Winnipeg, a lawyer, a human resource specialist, an expert in finances and an expert in social development. Their main focus is to provide the Executive Director with direction in matters relating to all areas of the program. They also develop policies and procedures, oversee the diversion program and are responsible for managing fiscal administration.

The Broken-Spirited Relations
The "broken spirit" is the term used to describe the Aboriginal offender. In the discussions leading up to the development of the program, it was decided to move away from the common terms of

"offender" and "victim" to a term that more adequately reflects the spiritual aspect of Aboriginal traditions drawn upon by the Aboriginal Ganootamaage Justice Services of Winnipeg, Inc. It was also decided that the term used should express the prevailing nature of the problems exhibited by most of the Aboriginal offenders. That is, they appear to be spiritually bankrupt, which can result in a loss of continuity and balance in their lives. On the other hand, the broken-spirited relations refers to both the Aboriginal offender and the victim. It is a term that perhaps best describes one major focus of the program which is to heal or mend the spirit of both the offender and the victim.

The Crown
The Crown Attorney includes the attorneys acting on behalf of the Crown. The role of the Crown is to identify and divert the broken spirit from the main justice proceedings by means of a referral to AGJSW. The system utilized by the Crown to determine who is eligible for referral consists of an evaluation of the charge and the circumstances of the offence. A list of a number of offences that are not eligible for diversion are used in this evaluation. These offences include: driving offences, such as refusing a breathalyzer; criminal negligence and dangerous or impaired driving; sexual offences and domestic violence (child abuse, spousal and/or partner abuse). If the circumstances of the alleged offence were serious in nature and involved violence, personal injury, weapons, a potentially dangerous situation or theft over $5000, the Crown Attorney may prefer court proceedings. The offences that are eligible include theft under $5000, mischief under (destruction of property valued at under $5000), property damage, common assault, obtaining goods through crime and joy riding. Equally or more important, to be eligible for AGJSW the broken spirit must admit responsibility for their wrongdoing.

Aboriginal Court Workers
Originally it was envisioned that the Aboriginal court workers would play a large role in identifying the individuals for the program. Their role has, however, proven to be quite limited; currently they only distribute AGJSW pamphlets to Aboriginal offenders. In any case, once the Crown makes the referral, AGJSW has full authority to sentence each individual so referred.

The Community Council
The community council includes supporters of the broken-spirited relations (both the broken spirit and the victim), as well as positive role models from the Aboriginal, Metis and non-Aboriginal communities. The broken spirits may choose any supporters they wish. Usually these supporters consist of two to three family members or friends selected by the broken spirit. The role of the community council is to participate in the development of a holistic healing plan that might include some or all of the following methods: healing through drug and alcohol treatment centres, spiritual and cultural teachings, community service and/or restitution. All of these are intended to aid the individual in learning self-respect and modifying her/his behaviour.

The Community Council Coordinator (CCC)
The Community Council Coordinator is the first person the broken spirit encounters at AGJSW: the coordinator does intake and assesses the broken spirits, and acts as a liaison with the Crown Attorney's office, Aboriginal court workers, various legal representatives, Aboriginal Services Agencies, Youth Correction Center staff and the Winnipeg Police Service. To do this, the CCC supports and sometimes "speaks for" the broken spirit in all necessary interactions. The liaison work also consists of keeping everyone apprised of all relevant information pertaining to the broken spirit's progress and eventual completion of the healing plan.

The CCC also facilitates the Community Council Forums, the meetings where the formation and delivery of the healing plan occurs. These meetings are referred to as circles in many Aboriginal societies and are the major component of the diversion process. Another very important aspect of the CCC's position involves monitoring the progress of the healing plan for each broken spirit, throughout the entire process.

The CCC for Aboriginal Ganootamaage Justice Services of Winnipeg must have a deep understanding of the problems encountered by the broken spirit, especially those pertaining to the criminal justice system. As with all other staff members in this program, she or he must have an in-depth knowledge of the effects of colonization on Aboriginal peoples. Some of these effects include: substance abuse, low self-esteem, lack of adequate parenting skills, poor education, and the underlying problem of loss of cultural traditions and cultural identity. (See York, 1990; Lee, 1992 for extensive discussion of these dynamics.) Most notably, these effects are thought to arise from involvement in the residential school system and the child welfare system. Indeed, all broken spirits who have come to AGJSW to date, with the exception of two individuals, have been involved in the child welfare system. The CCC utilizes her/his knowledge of the effects of colonization along with a holistic approach in all interventions made on behalf of the broken spirits.

The Elder
The role of the Elder involves an eclectic approach that has existed in Aboriginal communities for centuries. It encompasses many and varied roles in areas such as peacemaking, ceremonial facilitating, healing and the delivery of traditional teachings. An Elder is recognized as such on the basis of his or her contributions to Aboriginal communities and all humanity. Elders are gifted persons who have dealt with a lot of life experiences and, if need be, they have gone through extensive healing processes so that they have reached a stage of life where they are in a position to pass along their wisdom to others. These experiences are pertinent given the extraordinary history of Aboriginal people. Each Elder, being an individual first, brings his or her own unique gifts to the community. Elders are specialized through their life experiences and educational backgrounds to deal with issues in a variety of areas such as justice, alcohol and drug abuse, family violence and physical health issues. An Elder is a peacemaker and leader who has the ability to greatly influence the community. Above all, Elders are compassionate human beings who offer their gifts to all people. The current resident Elder at AGJSW exemplifies these qualities. He has an impressive background and possesses qualifications received from many cultures. Some of these qualifications that reflect the mainstream culture include being an electrician, a learned archaeologist and an anthropologist. He also has been gifted with the ability to receive visions from the spirit world that guide him in his teachings. Perhaps his most striking characteristic is his ability to feel and assess the needs of others. Most recently, AGJSW acquired the presence of a woman Elder; as a result, approximately half of the broken spirits referred to the diversion program are female. The addition of this Elder has enhanced the services provided to the female broken spirits, who feel more comfortable dealing with some issues with a female. The Elder facilitates some Community Council Forums as well as the women's healing circles and sweat-lodge ceremonies. She works one day a

week and also provides individual counselling for the female broken spirits if needed.

The Elder's role in the diversion process encompasses many areas but focuses mainly on the healing process. Along with the CCC, he or she participates in the ongoing assessments of the broken spirits entering the program and in the development of their healing plan. The Elder also leads participants in all Aboriginal traditional ceremonies necessary to the program.

Aboriginal Ganootamaage Justice Services of Winnipeg Process
The Aims

The intent of the diversion process is to divert Aboriginal criminal offenders from the regular court system and to provide holistic supports that address some of the special needs of Aboriginal offenders. The process is complex and involves the interaction of the many individuals spoken of above. In addition, AGJSW also has a number of support programs set up to enhance the quality and accessibility of the diversion program. These programs include both the use of volunteers and public education initiatives.

A holistic approach that takes into consideration the entire realm of an individual's life, is evident throughout the whole program. The central theme of an Aboriginal value system promotes respect for all people, animal, places and things. This holistic approach should not be confused with religious approaches that sometimes offer a narrow viewpoint on life and may only be available to those who share the same belief system. An Aboriginal holistic approach should be viewed as a way of life that is deeply spiritual and inclusive in nature, in that it respects all people, no matter what their belief system is. In keeping with this tradition, if a broken spirit does not want to participate in the Aboriginal traditional methods because of conflicting beliefs, they can still utilize the program. All of the broken spirits who are referred to the program are asked their particular religious belief and are given the option to not participate in the traditional ceremonies. The issue of conflicting religious beliefs, however, has not arisen to date: all broken spirits have been open to experiencing Aboriginal holistic traditional methods.

Since the inception of the program in January 1998, 161 individuals have been referred to AGJSW. The demographic information on these individuals indicates that over 55 percent were single, 55 percent had an FPS file, 45 percent had some high school, 51 percent were on social assistance, 52 percent were female, 48 percent were male. Half of the broken spirits were less than thirty years old. The characteristics of cases referred include: shoplifting (59), mischief under (destruction of property valued at under $5000) (20), other thefts and frauds under $5000 (17), other property crimes, such as joy riding (15); crimes against the person, such as assault (41); causing a disturbance (7). Some of the most common offences committed by the broken spirits include shoplifting, theft over $200 and joy riding. Each individual participated in the development and fulfilment of a healing plan. The healing plan consists of the individual's involvement in various Aboriginal traditional ceremonies such as healing circles, sweat-lodge ceremonies, smudges, feasts, pipe ceremonies and powwows. The overall purpose of the program is to facilitate healing utilizing Aboriginal traditions, so that the offender and victim come together and form a more harmonious relationship. The healing needed to mend this relationship is thought to ultimately affect all areas of the Aboriginal broken spirit's life; it enhances total well-being and reduces the likelihood of balance being broken again.

Most interactions are generally of an informal nature. The ceremonies, however, are carried out more formally, respecting the traditions that have been passed down through generations. All individuals involved play very important roles in the process. The broken-spirited relations are, however, considered to be of prime importance and are treated accordingly. Although the CCC, the Elder and the executive director are involved, the underlying philosophy stresses an egalitarian system in which everyone is treated equitably. The result is that the inputs of all concerned resonate throughout the entire process.

Developing Trust
One of the most striking examples of the implementation of a holistic approach is revealed in the Elder and CCC's approach to the intake process. It is a non-bureaucratic, personal and comprehensively detailed system that exists to serve the community. The holistic approach is designed to avoid the treatment of broken spirits in the bureaucratic manner which often occurs in the mainstream justice system. Therefore, respecting Aboriginal cultural traditions, an emphasis is placed on the whole individual so that the broken spirit's mind, body, spirit and soul are considered in the process.

The referrals to the diversion program are received mainly from the Crown Attorney's office. The CCC regularly attends the courthouse on a weekly basis to liaise with court workers, hear cases and receive referrals. On rare occasions, referrals come from legal aid lawyers or directly from the police. As well, referrals from the community, the family, self-referrals and walk-ins are accepted.

With few exceptions, all referrals received from the Crown are accepted. Initially, some concern was expressed in regard to accepting solvent abusers into the program because it was thought that the nature of their problems were such that they might not be able to carry out the responsibilities of the healing plan. They were accepted, however, and approximately half have been cooperative, and have been able to adjust and work with their healing plan. In terms of AGJSW's criteria for intake, the broken spirit must admit his or her responsibility for the offence and must agree to participate in the healing process. The broken spirits who have been injured by the offender have the option to participate in the healing circles as well. The CCC explains the diversion program to the victims and invites them to participate if they so wish. To date, only one victim has participated in the process: this may relate to the fact that most offences (such as shoplifting) have not been committed against individuals, but against large corporations. In these cases large corporations may not want to expend the time and money required to participate in the diversion process. The newness of the program and lack of understanding regarding the benefits of the program may also account for this discrepancy.

Once the referral is received, a meeting is set between the broken spirit and the CCC. This meeting marks the beginning of a spiritual, intellectual, emotional and sometimes physical healing process for the broken spirit. The primary purpose of the first meeting is to obtain demographic information and prepare the case history of the broken spirit. During this process, an intricate stage of events occurs in which the CCC and the broken spirit get to know each other through the disclosure and interchange of personal information. In this way, a relationship of trust is developed.

AGJSW is thoroughly described during this initial trust-building stage. The description includes an explanation of the process in which the healing plan is constructed, and details of the healing plan and circles with a special emphasis placed upon the responsibilities of the broken spirit. The voluntary nature of the program is also emphasized. This is done so that the individual need not feel forced into the program, thereby assuring greater participation and commitment to the healing process. In describing the program criteria, the CCC emphasizes the flexibility of the program, for example, any special schedule needs such as those required for school or job purposes, will be accommodated. The broken spirit is also told of all her/his options and is made aware of the fact that the Crown requires feedback on the progress throughout the diversion process.

The entire intake process can take one to three meetings depending on the individual. More time may be needed to prepare an extremely shy and withdrawn broken spirit for the healing process. This may include a preliminary meeting with the Elder or Community Council Coordinator for the Community Council Forum. In that case, the broken spirit is provided with the opportunity to talk about fears related to participating in the forum. Overall, the intake process is not a rigid system: a flexible, holistic approach is utilized. This method further aids the development of a trust relationship by reinforcing the fact that someone sincerely cares about the broken spirit.

A good portion of the assessment of the broken spirit, in terms of suitability to the program, is done by the CCC as part of the intake process. A meeting with the Elder also takes place for assessment purposes. The Elder utilizes intuitive methods rather than formal assessment to make his judgements. The assessment considers the broken spirit's willingness to commit to healing and their current state of well-being, both of which influence their ability to complete the healing plan.

The Healing Plan
The healing plan is a contract developed by means of a general consensus among all the parties involved, referred to collectively as the Community Council Forum. The Community Council Forum is comprised of supporters of the broken-spirited relations, positive role models from the Aboriginal, Metis, and non-Aboriginal communities, the CCC and the Elder(s). The primary focus of the Community Council Forum is to facilitate healing and growth, rather than punishment for a wrongdoing. The Community Council suggests a number of options for achieving this outcome, such as participating in healing circles, attending health and wellness groups, community service and participating in various Aboriginal ceremonies.

The uniqueness of this method lies in the fact that the person who commits the crime is given the opportunity to contribute to his or her healing process rather than having a sentence imposed by a judge as a means of punishment and restitution. In the event that the broken spirit does not comply with the planned healing process, she/he can be reverted to the mainstream justice system. Forty-four cases were referred back to the crown, including those who had not shown up for their referral meeting, had been difficult to locate, or had not successfully completed a healing plan.

The healing plan implements traditional Aboriginal teachings intended to lead the broken spirit on a path of self-discovery. The plan depends on the information derived from the initial assessment and is individualized to suit the needs of each broken spirit, although it has been noted that most broken spirits have essentially similar problems. Most notably, the broken spirits usually come to the program in a state of disorientation and great despair resulting from damage to their minds, hearts, bodies and spirits. It is thought that this damage may have been inflicted on them by mainstream systems that discriminate against Aboriginal peoples. These factors must be mentioned in order to better understand the structure and content of the healing plan.

Traditional Healing
In keeping with a holistic approach, the healing plan also attempts to address the physical need of cleansing the body of unwanted irritants. Traditional healing medicines are sometimes used depending on the particular needs of the broken spirit. As a result of the multidimensional damage to the Aboriginal self, the broken spirit usually has resorted to some form of substance abuse in order to numb the pain. The first step of the healing plan often involves ridding the system of toxins; the Elder prescribes traditional medicines to help the broken spirit feel well physically. The traditional medicines recommended by the AGJSW's Elder consist of between forty and sixty plants and herbs.

These medicines have been hand-picked in the bush by the Elder and his helpers throughout the summer. Knowledge of the uses of these plants has been taught to the Elder by other Elders through many generations. Some of this traditional knowledge has also been obtained through the gift of visions. All traditional medicines have also been extensively tested by the AGJSW Elder. The ingestion of combinations of various plants rids the body of unhealthy toxins, through expulsion of sweat and mucous, leaving the broken spirit more ready to face the difficult task of confronting his emotional, spiritual and intellectual ills.

The sweat-lodge ceremony is another cleansing method used in the diversion program. This ceremony is an important part of the program as it not only allows the broken spirit to participate in cultural ceremonial practices but also allows the broken spirit to symbolically drive out negative inner forces leaving room for future growth. The ceremony involves the broken spirit, the Elder and other participants entering a circular, hut-like structure known as a sweat-lodge. In past generations, the sweat-lodge was made of twigs covered by animal skins. Presently, most sweat-lodges are made of poles and tarp. Rocks are heated in a fire outside the sweat-lodge, then taken into the lodge and placed in a pit in the centre of the structure. The Elder or the facilitator of the sweat also brings water into the lodge and pours it over the hot rocks, to develop the steam and heat which produces a sweat.

Aboriginal traditions rely on the sweat-lodge ceremony in order to help cleanse the heart, body, mind and soul. The rocks heated for the sweats are seen as animate objects that have life and spirit. The burning of the rocks for use in sweat-lodge ceremonies facilitates the movement of the rock spirit into the broken spirit and other participants. This revives the spirit of all individuals involved in the sweat. The element of fire, used for heating the rocks, and the element of water, used to produce the sweat, are also seen as animate objects. Together, they cleanse the body and mind. Once the rocks are used for a sweat-lodge ceremony, they cannot be used again and are placed in such a manner as to distinguish them from rocks that have not been used for ceremonial purposes.

Presently, the Elders conduct approximately one sweat-lodge ceremony a week and have helpers who aid them in conducting the ceremony. In some cases, the broken spirit has to be taken to the sweat-lodge three or four times before she/he is ready to continue on in the healing process. Not surprisingly, this takes a great deal of time. In order for the program to realize its full potential, other Elders or Elder's helpers are needed. Presently, the program has two Elder's helpers but this is proving to be insufficient even at this early stage of the program. It will not be known until the end of the three year pilot period whether more helpers will be added.

Circles—The Heart of AGJSW

Aboriginal traditional circles are found in every healing plan. The circle is symbolic of a holistic philosophy; it is a tool used to illustrate Aboriginal people's beliefs in the circularity of life, and helps to convey the connections and relationships with the Creator and all creations. There are many different dimensions to the concept of circles. They not only provide a framework in establishing arenas for relating to one another, but also provide a framework for shaping perception and interpretations of the world. For example, the principle of a circle expresses the need for an equilibrium among mind, body, spirit and emotions in order to maintain physical and psychological well-being. It can also relate to the need for a connection to the environment. The circle symbolically represents many areas of life: the cycle of birth and rebirth, seasonal change, growth and regrowth and a mirror that reflects oneself.

Perhaps most of the healing takes place within circles. When the broken spirits reach a point where they are ready for further healing, they may take part in talking, sharing, teaching and healing circles. Each type of circle is essentially similar in structure and is conducted with respect for all Aboriginal traditions. An example of this respect is the restriction of females from the circle when they have their moon-time (menstruation). Some Aboriginal traditions believe that a women's moon time is her most powerful time. Therefore, in order to prevent this power from interfering with other ceremonies, she must be doctored (red powder dotted on her forehead and the palms of her hands and feet) so that no harm comes to her. Another example of adherence to Aboriginal traditions is the purification, through burning of cedar, of the room where the circles take place. The ceiling of this room is circular also, this in keeping with Aboriginal traditions. In some circles, the individuals sit around a drum that is placed in the centre of the circle. The drum is sounded at the beginning and end of the circle. The drum sound represents the heartbeat and is sounded by the Elder or facilitator who offers a prayer to the Creator at the beginning and end of each circle.

The Creator is considered to be at the centre of all that exists. It is for this reason that opening and closing prayers giving thanks to the Creator are present in all circles and in all Aboriginal ceremonies. A smudging ceremony intended to purify the self occurs before the opening prayer. This ceremony involves spreading the smoke emitted from the burning of sage, sweet grass, tobacco or cedar over the head and heart. If anyone is uncomfortable with the smudging ceremony, they have the choice to excuse themselves from the circle until the ceremony is over or simply pass it by. An introduction of everyone participating in the circle follows. An eagle feather, a rock representing the Aboriginal grandmothers and grandfathers, or a talking stick may be brought into the circle. The passing of one of these objects indicates whose turn it is to speak. When the person is finished talking, it is then passed onto the next person. If the feather, rock or stick is not brought into the circle, then participants can speak or ask a question whenever they wish to do so.

The Elder or the facilitator of the circle encourages the seven teachings: Love, Humility, Courage, Respect, Honesty, Wisdom and Truth. These are the seven basic principles that have been passed down from generation to generation in most Aboriginal communities. The encouragement of these principles is done in order to build trust among the people in the circle. In the circle, the broken spirit is encouraged by the disclosures of others, who quite often have been in the same situation. This is done so that the broken spirits will eventually grow to feel safe enough to take responsibility for their own feelings.

The teaching circle utilizes many models that are basically geared to teaching the broken-spirit traditions and values of Aboriginal culture. The underlying principle of all teaching circles is the respect for self and all creations. An example of one lesson taught by the Elder at AGJSW is called "The ABCs." In this lesson, members of the circle are taught how an individual's mind, heart, body and soul are connected to Mother Earth, and each of these is specifically linked to a rock, tree, grass and animal. The rock-mind connection represents faith, shelter, power, control and compassion. The tree-heart connection represents honesty, strength and warmth. The body-grass connection stands for kindness, health and growth. The soul-animal connection represents sharing, caring, love and forgiveness. Aboriginal traditional teachings specify that an imbalance will occur that can cause great disruption to the spirit if any of these areas are not respected. For example, if the heart and soul are neglected, then the individual may behave in a dishonest, unloving manner, that will in turn affect the mind and body. This holistic interconnectedness is emphasized in all the teachings, and is considered by the Elders to be of great importance and value to human beings.

The urbanization of large numbers of Aboriginal people has resulted in the loss of Aboriginal cultural identity. The Elder is cognizant of the fact, that for almost all broken spirits, this is the first time in their lives that they have had an opportunity to learn of, and engage in, Aboriginal traditions and ceremonies. It is also the first time many of the broken spirits have had any type of support in dealing with their problems. Therefore, the circles are individualized to suit the needs of the broken spirits; for example, co-ed as well as separate men's and women's circles may be used. The utilization of various circles is intended to help the broken spirit feel more comfortable when discussing issues that might be too difficult to discuss in the presence of the opposite sex, such as cases where a female broken spirit was victimized by a male or vice versa. The broken spirits take three to six months, on average, to complete their healing plans.

Other Traditional Ceremonies
Periodically the staff at AGJSW host a number of other Aboriginal traditional ceremonies that are not an integral part of the diversion process but are important components nonetheless. They provide further opportunity for the broken spirits to participate in Aboriginal ceremonies, thereby increasing their knowledge of the Aboriginal culture and enriching their mind and spirit. This in turn can precipitate further healing. These ceremonies include powwows and summer and winter solstice and the vernal equinox celebrations. All of these ceremonies consist of opening and closing prayers as well as some or all of the following: pipe ceremonies, sweat-lodge ceremonies, smudges to purify the self and physical area, feasts and tobacco, cloth and food offerings to the spirit world. The solstices and the equinox are very important times in Aboriginal culture. They represent time to acknowledge the difficulties Aboriginal peoples have gone through in the past, to pray for a better future for Aboriginals and all creations and to celebrate and give thanks to the spirit world.

The Volunteer Program
Virtually all key positions involved in the diversion process need volunteer support. To facilitate this, AGJSW has developed an extensive volunteer program that seeks to provide assistance to the broken spirits, staff members, the organization as a whole and the Aboriginal community. The CCC, the Elder and helpers require assistance with the Community Council Forums and implementation of the healing plans. This might entail assisting in the various circles, the cultural and traditional teachings, the sweat-lodge, feasts and ceremonies, and participating in the development of a healing plan or any other duties related to the Community Council Forums. Other areas of the program requiring volunteer assistance include: special events (for example, Powwows, conferences and workshops), office support (for example, answering telephones, mailing and typing) and public education (for example, scheduling and preparing material for outreach presentations).

In order to assess the skills and qualifications of each volunteer, the coordinator administers a series of interviews and questionnaires to determine where the volunteer will best fit in the program. The interviews and questionnaires contain items pertaining to work-related and life experiences that indicate the potential volunteers' knowledge of Aboriginal culture, communication skills, office skills, etc. Then an orientation meeting is held where volunteers are given further information on the diversion program. Each volunteer is asked to observe a Community Council Forum in order to get first-hand experience in a circle. A meeting then takes place in which the volunteer is given information relating to their specific duties.

All volunteer participation is supervised by a staff member in a holistic manner. The volunteer is active in the area that relates most closely to the skills that she or he possesses. Aboriginal and non-Aboriginal individuals are encouraged to volunteer. While the volunteer program provides much needed assistance to AGJSW, it also provides volunteers with the opportunity to develop skills and gain experience in a diversion program. Currently the volunteer program has approximately eighty general members who help out occasionally on such events as the annual Elders' gathering, feasts and spring equinox celebrations. As well, twenty-five volunteers regularly participate in the community council forums and help around the office when needed. The volunteers have contributed over 1000 hours of work to AGJSW.

Public Education Component

Perhaps one of the most important aspects of the program is informing the public of its existence. The Public Education Coordinator prepares and coordinates the distribution of program materials that describe all aspects of AGJSW and presents these materials through an outreach program. Extensive publicizing of the program is done to ensure that everyone who can benefit from AGJSW knows about it. It is also done to make the public aware of the valuable and hard work that is taking place in the Aboriginal community to address the high rate of Aboriginal involvement in criminal activities. Publicity materials include brochures, a quarterly newsletter, overheads, press releases, radio and television announcements and various presentational handouts.

The newsletter, titled "Ganootamaage" (speaking for) contains the logo, developed by Aboriginal artist George Delorme, which consists of a circle divided into four sections. The circle represents the circle of life. The four sections represent the four directions, north, east, south and west, and the four "races" of the world, depicted by the colors red, black, yellow and white. Superimposed on the circle is the gavel of justice and an eagle feather. The eagle feather symbolizes truth, an underlying principle found in every aspect of Aboriginal life.

The newsletter presents information and educational articles relating to the criminal justice system and to activities of AGJSW. These articles are submitted by staff members, community members and others. They might include reports on topics such as the first broken spirit to finish a healing plan, conferences attended by staff members, fund-raising events or personal profiles of staff and Aboriginal community members.

Two pamphlets describe the volunteer program and the Community Council Diversion program. One brochure outlines the volunteer recruitment process and the areas of volunteer interest. The second brochure describes the referral and diversion process, including a brief overview of AGJSW and of restorative justice models. Both of these pamphlets have been widely distributed.

Media avenues other than print have also been utilized. An advertisement has been presented on an Aboriginal radio station, NCI (Native Communications Inc.), in Winnipeg, and a public service announcement for television was featured on Videon Cable 11. Additional radio and television advertisements are planned for the future. The main activity of the public education coordinator is informational presentations to various Aboriginal and non-Aboriginal organizations in Winnipeg. To do this involves networking and collaborating with various organizations in order to reach as many people as possible.

Conclusion

Aboriginal Ganootamaage Justice Services of Winnipeg (AGJSW) has a comprehensive array of programs that provide services to Aboriginal offenders diverted from the mainstream justice system. The services provided utilize Aboriginal cultural traditions as well as the incorporation of contemporary organizational practices that do not impinge on cultural traditions. All services use a holistic approach that emphasizes a consideration of all things affecting all parts of the individual. This humanistic approach is flexible and informal, allowing for a personal, less bureaucratic involvement. The fact that many broken spirits visit AGJSW upon completion of their healing plan suggests that, in the short time AGJSW has been operating, the staff have touched the lives of many in a profound way.

The services provided by AGJSW have been expanded in the last year to include the participation of AGJSW staff in two sentencing circles. The sentencing circles operate under basically the same principles and procedures as the diversion process, except that a Court of Queen's Bench judge makes the final decision, and the crimes heard are more serious in nature. For example, the charges in the two sentencing circles in which AGJSW participated pertained to drunk driving causing death. It is anticipated that involvement in sentencing circles will increase in the future.

Unfortunately some problems have arisen regarding certain areas of AGJSW. In terms of the diversion process, only one *victim* has participated in the healing process to date. Perhaps one of the reasons for this dilemma, as previously discussed, is that most of the victims to date have been large retail corporations. The newness of the program might also be a factor. However, if the program is going to address its intended need, that is to heal the broken-spirited relations, then a closer look at this factor is required.

Healing plans take from six weeks to three months to complete. Many broken spirits, however, maintain contact with the AGJSW by taking part in volunteer initiatives and by participating in the traditional ceremonies that are not part of their healing plans but provide further healing.

A formal evaluation of the program is currently being carried out by an outside organization. Because of limited resources, actual follow-up is not carried out by AGJSW; instead, the Crown Attorney's office provides the names of individuals who have re-offended. Preliminary results indicate that 156 broken spirits, approximately 1.5 percent of participants, who have been referred to AGJSW as of January, 2000, have re-offended. It should be noted, however, that because AGJSW is only a three-year pilot project with the end-date fast approaching, the follow-up period has been relatively short in some cases. Nonetheless, these early results are encouraging.

The evaluation also involves a review of all documentation relating to AGJSW, as well as interviews with key members, Elders and program staff. The documentation review includes an examination of budgets from AGJSW, the Winnipeg Police Service, Legal Aid Clinic and Manitoba Justice, in order to determine if the program is cost-effective. A roundtable discussion involving program staff, police, Department of Justice and Department of Finance officials has already taken place. The preliminary results of the evaluation indicate that AGJSW clearly addresses the objective of reducing the rate of incarceration and recidivism among Aboriginal people in Winnipeg, thereby reducing costs to the mainstream justice system. Since AGJSW is the first program of its kind in Winnipeg and has been operating for a short period of time, it is not yet possible to accurately predict whether it will have a significant effect on statistics relating to the criminal justice system.

However, community members have indicated that they are most concerned with improvements in the lives of the broken spirits and their families, rather than with reducing the number of Aboriginal offenders in the justice system, as important as that goal may be. The Community Council Coordinator, as well as other workers, give many hours of their own time, engaging in activities with the broken spirits to facilitate healing. This factor makes it is easy to predict that AGJSW will have a positive effect on the quality of life to those individuals it is able to touch through its services. One major positive effect that is difficult to measure, but has been reported by program staff, is that most broken spirits state that they feel much better about themselves, knowing that at least someone cares about their well-being. Statements such as this imply an increase in feelings of self-worth for the broken spirits. In turn, improved self-esteem can lead to improved family and community relations, thereby helping to reduce incidences of domestic and other violence and child and drug abuse which, as previously mentioned, are prevalent in the Aboriginal community. However, it can take years for the broken spirits to fully integrate the lessons they have learned from Aboriginal cultural traditions into their lives. Perhaps the greatest contribution of the AGJSW is the introduction of Aboriginal cultural traditions into the broken spirits' lives. This not only encourages spiritual, physical, intellectual and emotional healing for the broken spirits, but also provides cultural enrichment for staff, volunteers and all individuals who have encounters with Aboriginal Ganootamaage Justice Services of Winnipeg.

Note

1. The authors thank Pamela J. Marsden for her assistance with writing this chapter.

Chapter 5

Striving Towards Balance:
A Blended Treatment/Healing Approach with Aboriginal Sexual Offenders
Lawrence A. Ellerby

Traditional Aboriginal culture and healing is enjoying a resurgence. Individuals, communities and governments are returning to cultural teachings to find solutions to many societal concerns. Across Canada provincial and federal Corrections are developing and implementing programs specifically designed for Aboriginal offenders.

As a treatment program providing institutional and community-based sexual offender treatment to a high proportion of Aboriginal men, the Native Clan Organization's Forensic Behavioral Management Clinic has attempted to develop and deliver programming that is culturally appropriate while at the same time addressing risk and risk management. By creating a treatment team comprised of clinicians and spiritual helpers we have attempted to synthesize aspects of contemporary sexual offender treatment and traditional cultural and spiritual healing. We refer to this as a "blended" treatment/healing approach. The term blended is used to reflect that treatment and healing are fundamentally interconnected and equally important interventions, which are delivered in an integrated manner.

The blended treatment/healing model was developed out of a desire to meet the needs of Aboriginal men in our program who did not respond to contemporary strategies for the treatment of sexual-offending behaviour. This modified approach has engaged many of the men who struggled in, or were resistant to, contemporary programming. Attending to cultural issues and incorporating healing practices into sexual offender treatment has facilitated the process of change and supported men to work towards balance in their lives. Ultimately, this diminishes risk and contributes to the fundamental goal of sexual offender treatment, enhancing community safety and contributing to community wellness.

The Evolution of the Blended Approach

When the clinic began providing treatment services to adult males who had engaged in sexual-offending behaviour in 1987, we offered a cognitive-behavioural, relapse prevention program, as this was the intervention identified as "best practice" in this field.[1] Although we sensed that some of the Aboriginal men in our program might have treatment needs beyond or different from this approach, we were not sure what these needs would be or how best to address them. In an effort to enhance the program's ability to serve these men, the clinical team was open to learning about cultural issues and to considering how cultural factors might influence the way in which some individuals present themselves in and respond to treatment. In addition, based on cultural information, treatment was modified in an effort to make the experience more engaging and effective. For example, the level of challenging and confrontation was tempered, oral versus written exercises were assigned, stories and metaphors were integrated into the treatment process, and specific topics of interest, such as colonization and racism, became part of the content of treatment (for further details see Ellerby and Stonechild, 1998). These efforts represented attempts to address the needs of Aboriginal men in the program and reflected the first steps in moving towards a blended approach.

A culmination of factors led to expanding beyond these initial efforts to formally developing a culturally appropriate component to our program. Firstly, as a program situated in Winnipeg, Manitoba, we were aware that a large number of our clients would be Aboriginal as the prairie provinces (Manitoba, Saskatchewan and Alberta) have the largest representation of Aboriginal inmates in Canada and the highest proportion of Aboriginal sexual offenders (LaPrairie, 1996; LeClair, 1996; Motiuk and Belcourt, 1996). Secondly, we began to identify trends that appeared to differentiate the Aboriginal and non-Aboriginal men in our program. For example, issues of abandonment, displacement, racism and an absence or confusion of identity were more prominent among the Aboriginal men. In addition, compared to the non-Aboriginal men in the program the Aboriginal men tended to present with more pronounced histories of chronic exposure to maltreatment and abuse, substance abuse, poverty and death

(Ellerby, 1994). Finally, a review of our treatment outcome data suggested some differences in the response to treatment between Aboriginal and non-Aboriginal participants. While Aboriginal and non-Aboriginal men who completed our treatment program benefited equally (in reference to recidivism rates), Aboriginal men were far less likely to successfully complete treatment. They had a higher drop-out rate, were more frequently suspended and returned to prison and had a higher rate of re-offending sexually while still in treatment compared to the non-Aboriginal men (Ellerby, 1994).

In considering this information it was apparent that a sub-group of Aboriginal men participating in our program had distinct needs that required consideration and attention. As well, it appeared that for some Aboriginal men, a cognitive-behavioural approach was neither engaging nor meaningful. If the best practice interventions were not effective for some Aboriginal men then the treatment program was certainly not helping these particular individuals address their deficit areas or diminish their risk to re-offend. In response to this, our program looked to find a better way to reach and connect with these men. To accomplish this we sought the guidance of spiritual helpers: Native Spiritual Elders and individuals given the gift of the pipe.[2] In sharing thoughts about treatment, healing and facilitating the process of change, we saw that there could be a benefit in providing culturally appropriate healing along with specific sexual offender treatment interventions. While we were aware of the obvious differences between contemporary treatment and traditional healing, it became evident that when the shared objective is to help people grow and move towards wellness and harmony, the two approaches could work beautifully together, complementing and strengthening each other. These discussions led us to invite a Spiritual Elder to join our treatment team and to begin the process of learning how to integrate these two different yet complementary paths to change.

Since this time the clinic has employed various practices in an effort to find the best balance in blending treatment and healing. As a dynamic and continually evolving model the developmental process has offered wonderful new insights and directions to support the process of change, growth and risk management for men in treatment. It has, however, also presented frustrations and obstacles to be resolved.

Today we still continue to learn, modify and adapt our approach. While the means of blending treatment and healing continues to develop, the philosophy behind the model, supporting men to learn, grow and heal as a means of risk management, remains the same and has in fact strengthened over time.

Expanding Paradigms: Holism, Wellness and Spirituality

In working with Aboriginal spiritual helpers, we as clinicians came to recognize that a number of fundamental beliefs associated with healing were consistent with our clinical practice. Specific concepts of healing that immediately resonated with our treatment philosophy and approach were that of holism and wellness. Appreciating the significance of spirituality came later.

After considering some of the teachings we had learned and relating them to our existing practice we decided to expand our theoretical orientation. We moved from identifying our practice as cognitive-behavioural relapse prevention to seeing it as more consistent with a holistic paradigm (Ellerby, Bedard and Chartrand, in press).

There are a number of assumptions within holistic perspectives that fit well with our approach to treatment and that define the blended model. The first was the need to recognize the men we work with as whole individuals rather than primarily or exclusively as "sexual offenders." This perspective has significant implications. If offenders are viewed as whole human beings, the need to work with them in a compassionate and respectful manner is highlighted. As well, this position emphasizes the need to not only address offence-specific issues, but to attend to other relevant areas of men's lives in the treatment/healing process. The need to expand beyond cognitive-behavioural interventions also becomes apparent. Within a holistic orientation it is the pursuit of balance between the mental, spiritual, emotional and physical dimensions of a person that leads to awareness and healing (Bopp and Bopp, 1997; McGaa, 1990; Ross, 1996; Warry, 1998).

A holistic orientation not only looks at the person as a whole but attends to the interconnectedness of the individual, both internally (the connectedness of the mental, spiritual, emotional and physical dimensions within us) and externally (the connections to the people and world around us). As such, offenders can not be viewed in isolation but need to be considered in the larger context of their connections with others, such as their family and community and with the land or mother earth (Bopp and Bopp, 1997; Ellerby, Bedard and Chartrand, in press; Ellerby and Ellerby, 1998; Wyse and Thomasson, 1999). While we have always considered this in our practice, this traditional teaching has further emphasized the need to consider the men in treatment within a larger context and for their treatment/healing experience to reflect this.

Another paradigm shift that has influenced our practice is the movement away from a model of sickness to a model of wellness. This has resulted in a transition from focusing primarily on what the men in treatment must do in order to avoid re-offending to emphasizing what they need to do in order to live healthy, well-balanced lives, so they are not at risk to re-offend. As well, the message has moved from focusing on the fact that there is no cure for sexual-offending behaviour (a tenet of the relapse prevention model) to stressing that change is both possible and probable if one works towards wellness (Bopp and Bopp, 1997; Ellerby, Bedard and Chartrand, in press).

Attending to spirituality has been another significant and fundamental shift in our program's philosophical orientation and clinical practice. Spirituality is typically a neglected area in clinical practice with forensic clients; however, it is the foundation of healing within traditional Aboriginal healing. Recently there has been growing attention to the relevance of addressing spirituality in the treatment of Aboriginal men who have engaged in sexual-offending behaviour (Ellerby, Bedard and Chartrand, in press; Fournier and Crey, 1997; Wyse and Thomasson, 1999). Attention to spirituality does not mean promoting religiosity. It simply recognizes a spiritual dimension within human beings and acknowledges many people's belief in a higher power. This acknowledgement allows people to discuss, explore and nurture their spiritual side as part of their overall treatment/healing experience.

It is important to state that while we have expanded our treatment philosophy, orientation and practice to encompass a holistic orientation, a wellness approach and attention to spirituality, we have not abandoned the essential elements of treatment to address inappropriate sexual behaviours. Within the blended model significant attention is given to discussing and addressing inappropriate sexual interests, thoughts/fantasies, arousal and behaviours in specific detail.

Delivering A Blended Treatment/Healing Model
The Helpers
In the blended model the clinical team is truly multidisciplinary. The team has consisted of clinicians and consultants from various back-

grounds including social work, psychology, psychiatry, and pipe carriers and spiritual Elders. The qualities of the helpers who make up the treatment team and deliver the blended treatment/healing model are essential to the success of this approach. Therapists and spiritual helpers must demonstrate a high level of openness, cooperation, respect, and a shared vision of this model and its objectives. They must also be willing to work collaboratively within a multidisciplinary team alongside team members with whom they might not normally work. It is likely that programs attempting to integrate contemporary treatment and traditional healing will struggle in providing an integrated model without cooperative and respectful working relationships between clinical treatment providers and traditional spiritual helpers.

While the role of counsellors or therapists is typically understood, the role of spiritual helpers in treatment programs is less clear. The role of the Elder on our team has been that of a teacher, advisor, counsellor and spiritual leader. While Elders are often viewed as cultural teachers, their primary function is that of healing, through traditional teachings and ceremony (for example, sweat-lodge ceremonies, pipe ceremonies, fasts). A detailed account of the role of Elders in our program and in other Aboriginal sexual offender treatment programs can be found in Ellerby and Ellerby (1998) and Ellerby and Stonechild, (1998).

In addition to Elders, pipe carriers have been important members of our treatment team. We have relied heavily on their knowledge and skills. The pipe carriers have typically served as a bridge between the clinicians and the Elders, helping each to better understand the other. While the clinicians are primarily grounded in contemporary sexual offender specific interventions, and the Elders are focused on traditional healing, the pipe carriers that have been part of our team have had traditional healing knowledge, counselling skills and training in sexual offender treatment.

The treatment/healing team consists of both male and female contemporary and traditional helpers. It is important for the men in treatment to have exposure to strong, healthy women who can be role models and help them work through what for many are their negative attitudes towards women and feelings of insecurity, inadequacy, anger, guilt and shame associated with females. Having male and female treatment/healing team members work together (for example, co-facilitating groups) is also an important part of the process as it allows the men in treatment to observe an equal, respectful and cooperative relationship between a male and female.

Given the unique composition of the team it is important that there are ongoing opportunities to discuss how the treatment/ healing process is unfolding and how the helpers are working together. Supervision meetings serve to focus on these issues as well as to discuss ideas related to program development, to problem solve difficult cases and to discuss how team members are managing the stressors associated with their work.

The Clients
The reference to working with men throughout is due to the fact that the vast majority of our clients are adult males. The clinic provides services to both Aboriginal and non-Aboriginal men who have committed a range of sexual offences. These include men labelled or diagnosed as obscene telephone callers, exhibitionists, voyeurs, incest offenders, child molesters, pedophiles, rapists, rapist/pedophiles, sadistic sexual offenders and individuals who have committed murder with sexual overtones. We see a small number of men who are borderline or low in their intellectual functioning as well as a small number of men who have a mental health diagnosis (for example, manic-depression, depression, schizophrenia).

Not all of the men who attend the clinic participate in the blended treatment/ healing program, as this is one of two program streams available. The other, which is the contemporary sexual offender treatment program, has been influenced by the philosophies of the blended model; however, it is different and distinct. The contemporary program is facilitated by clinicians and is somewhat different in its content and process. For example, it does not include traditional rituals, teachings or ceremonies. As well, while spirituality has become incorporated in the contemporary program, in contrast to the blended program it is not focused on as the fundamental dimension of healing.

The blended program is offered only for those individuals who wish to be involved in traditional healing. This voluntary participation is important because our experience has shown that only a small proportion of Aboriginal offenders choose to participate in traditional healing. This is consistent with previous findings suggesting that many Aboriginal offenders are satisfied participating in mainstream correctional programs and believe that these programs are of value and meet their needs (LePraire, 1996).

It is also worth noting that there are a small number of non-

Aboriginal men who are drawn to traditional healing. Those non-Aboriginal men with a genuine interest in pursuing traditional healing are welcome to take part in the blended program.

The Modalities of the Blended Program

Men participating in the blended program may be involved in a variety of treatment/ healing modalities including individual counselling, group therapy, sharing circles, sweat-lodge ceremonies, arousal modification sessions, couple counselling and community outreach support. The number of treatment/healing modalities in which individuals participate and the frequency and duration of their participation is individually determined based on the individual's level of risk, need and stability.

All men are assigned a primary helper and participate in individual counselling. This counselling may be provided by therapists familiar with cultural healing, or by a pipe carrier familiar with sexual offender treatment. In some cases an Elder will provide counselling. At times individual sessions are co-facilitated. The co-facilitating pairs vary and have included combinations of a therapist and an Elder, a therapist and a pipe carrier and a pipe carrier and an Elder. These co-facilitated sessions allow for issues discussed to be addressed from both a contemporary and a traditional point of view.

Group therapy is an important component of sexual offender treatment. Within the context of a group experience men learn they are not alone in the problems they have faced. As well, the group serves as a place of accountability. Men who engage in inappropriate sexual behaviour tend to deny, minimize and distort their account of their offending behaviour. Group members use their own experiences and insights to challenge and hold each other responsible for their offending. Within the group, men work together to facilitate greater openness and accountability, to develop insight into their offending and to work towards change.

In many ways the blended group is similar to the contemporary group; however, there are some significant distinguishing features. Rather than being facilitated by two therapists, the blended group is facilitated by a therapist, a pipe carrier and at times an Elder. As well, the process of the blended group differs in some aspects as traditional rituals, teachings and ceremonies are incorporated into the group. For example, each group begins with the burning of the sacred plants (tobacco, cedar, sweet grass and sage) and the smudging of the group members and facilitators. This is a purification ritual that prepares individuals for the healing that will occur within the group. A prayer to the Creator is offered upon the completion of the smudging and then the group begins.

During the course of a group session members have the option of holding an eagle feather, a talking stone or a talking stick to give them strength as they speak and to encourage honesty and depth in what they share. Unlike a sharing circle, individuals are allowed and encouraged to ask questions, challenge and provide feedback to the person speaking.

Some of the men in the blended program also participate in a sharing circle. A pipe carrier, an Elder or both facilitate this circle. In the circle the men are able to speak about whatever they would like to share. The individual holding the feather, stone or stick speaks until he is finished and then passes to the next person in the circle. When speaking in the sharing circle, people are not interrupted, questioned or challenged. They may receive feedback, but only through another person sharing when it is their turn in the circle. The provision of the sharing circle allows for a more traditional healing experience than group therapy provides. Because of the different process, style of interaction and greater attention to rituals, ceremonies and teachings some men find this process more comfortable. At times men are more open to share and disclose information about themselves and their lives as well as more willing to listen. It is not unusual for men to begin the process of becoming more open and genuine in the sharing circle and then generalize these gains to other aspects of their treatment/healing (for example, individual counselling, group therapy).

Participation in the sweat-lodge ceremony is another significant aspect of the blended treatment/healing approach. This is one of the most important and sacred ceremonies (for a detailed account of the sweat-lodge ceremony see Ross, 1992 and Ellerby and Stonechild, 1998). Elders describe the sweat-lodge ceremony as a place where the defensive walls of an individual can be broken down. The ceremony is about purification and individuals are said to be cleansed from the inside out. This allows for people to talk in an open, genuine and personal way, letting out feelings such as anger, pain and shame that have been buried inside. The sweat-lodge ceremony also helps bring clarity to one's thinking. It is said to be a place of rebirth that encourages and inspires hope.

We have been fortunate in our program to work with Elders who have focused the prayers in the sweat-lodge on topics relevant to the work done in individual and group sessions. For example, prayers and discussion in the sweat-lodge have included addressing personal issues such as anger, resentment, hate, jealousy, inadequacy, entitlement and shame. Elders have also addressed sexualized thinking, deviant sexual fantasies and attitudes towards women and children. Victim impact/empathy have been important issues raised by Elders during this ceremony. Elders have asked the men to consider and reflect on the harm done as a result of their offending and to pray for those whom they have hurt. Within ceremony Elders have stressed the importance of taking responsibility for changing one's life and for treating people with respect and kindness. The Elders also speak of the need to come to a place of forgiveness so one can let go of the negative feelings and thoughts that could potentially contribute to destructive behaviours, including offending.

On occasion the therapists involved in both the contemporary and blended programs will participate in sweat-lodge ceremonies with the men in the blended program. This is another way in which the interventions are integrated. It also provides an opportunity for the men to see and experience the mutual respect that exists amongst the traditional healers and contemporary treatment providers, both for each other and for what they each bring to the treatment/healing process.

Arousal modification is another component of the treatment/healing process. Some of the men in treatment have developed a sexual arousal response or a sexual preference for inappropriate forms of sexual behaviour. For example, they are sexually attracted to, and aroused by, children, or their sexual arousal is not inhibited by violence. These men must learn strategies to inhibit, control and modify their inappropriate sexual arousal and in some cases learn to develop arousal to appropriate consenting adult cues. This component of treatment is conducted in the clinic's phallometric laboratory. For men in the blended program, arousal modification sessions can be tailored to fit in with their healing. For example, in developing arousal control strategies, individuals in the blended program have used prayer, thoughts about traditional teachings and asking the Creator for strength as ways of assisting them to manage their arousal response to inappropriate cues.

For men who are in a committed relationship, couple counselling is encouraged. In these sessions, issues related to the individual's risk factors for offending and risk management strategies are shared with their partner so they can be an informed support person. As well, these sessions focus on relationship issues that may need attention. In addition, a partner support group is offered for spouses. The inclusion of men's partners in the treatment/healing process is seen to be important, particularly given the interconnectedness of the individual with his family and the importance of family in a holistic orientation.

Additional supports may be provided to men through the clinic's community outreach worker. The outreach worker assists men to integrate into the Winnipeg community upon their release from incarceration. This support is primarily provided to individuals who originate from rural or reserve communities but who are released on probation or parole to the city, as well as to high-risk and/or high-need individuals. Support is provided in a host of areas including, but not restricted to: providing assistance with deinstitutionalization and community adjustment, helping men familiarize themselves with the city, showing men how to use public transportation, finding appropriate and safe housing, providing guidance navigating through various social service agencies and government bureaucracies (for example, applying for social assistance, disability assistance, securing personal identification, applying for a treaty number), providing information and assistance in accessing training and employment programs, and helping men learn a range of life skills (for example, budgeting, shopping, problem-solving). This community outreach work extends support beyond the walls of the clinic and helps men deal with important everyday life tasks and responsibilities that they may not be familiar with or feel comfortable performing. This level of support responds to the multidimensionality of men and their needs, and recognizes the importance of assisting men to connect with and become part of the community.

The Teachings in a Blended Program

The teachings provided to men in the blended program are a combination of contemporary offence-specific teachings and traditional teachings. Some of the traditional teachings are specifically related to sexual-offending behaviour while others are more global lessons that are seen to be relevant and meaningful in facilitating risk management and wellness.

Offence-specific programming focuses on a wide range of issues. One area emphasized is the importance of self-disclosure, honesty and accountability. Men are encouraged to try to be open in discussing their life story so they can work towards a better understanding of themselves and the way they have functioned in their lives. Self-disclosure also allows the men to confront, work through and hopefully find a way to let go of the inner pain they carry as a result of their various life experiences. Disclosure involves the men discussing and working at being more authentic in relating the facts about their lives, with attention to areas such as their family of origin, developmental experiences, abuse history, relationships and history of destructive coping styles, particularly the acting out of inappropriate sexual behaviours.

This process of disclosure and learning lessons from the past to work towards change in the future has occasionally been an area of contention in the blended program. While many Elders strongly support this approach, we have encountered others who teach "the past is the past so move on." In consultation with spiritual helpers, the blended program has taken the position that while men in treatment must move forward from the past they need to do so in a "good way." This means learning what they can from past life patterns and bringing resolution to troubling issues they have carried with them through their lives.

This process of disclosure leads to another important offence-specific treatment goal or teaching, which is helping the men understand the pathways to offending. In this regard men learn to identify, recognize and understand the feelings, thoughts and behaviours that for them contribute to inappropriate sexual behaviour. These precursors make up what we call an "Unhealthy Life Cycle."

Within the Unhealthy Life Cycle poorly managed emotions are significant triggers that can lead to an escalation of destructive coping mechanisms and potentially to offending behaviours. As a result it is necessary for men to learn about their feelings and develop coping skills to manage feelings in a positive manner (for example, anger and depression management; assertiveness and communication training; bringing resolution to shame). Thoughts associated with an Unhealthy Life Cycle are typically negative cognitions directed at themselves, others and the world around them (for example, "I am stupid, ugly, no good," "I wish I was never born," "nobody cares about me," "you can't trust anyone" and "the world owes me"). Men are taught to recognize, challenge and replace negative attitudes, beliefs and thoughts/self-talk. They learn strategies for checking the validity of their self-statements and to reframe their thinking. Destructive styles of coping are also identified within the Unhealthy Life Cycle. Men identify the various ways in which they have attempted to cope in distorted and destructive ways (for example, substance abuse, social isolation, involvement in unhealthy peer and romantic relationships and aggression). The functional nature of these behaviours is challenged and alternative healthy coping strategies are developed. The link between general unhealthy styles of coping and sexual-offending behaviour is also examined.

The next part of the cycle we review with men is the "Crime Cycle." The Crime Cycle consists of the pattern of deviant sexual fantasies, cognitive distortions and planning that may be contributing factors to offending. Men learn about the role of inappropriate sexual thoughts, fantasy and arousal in offending and, if required, develop skills to modify deviant fantasies and arousal. They also learn to identify and challenge the distortions in thinking that minimize the seriousness and the inappropriate nature of sexual offending as well as their personal culpability. Such thinking styles include: denial, minimization (for example, "I only touched her once," "It's not that bad because I did not go all the way," "my victim was not harmed"), rationalization and justification (for example, "I would not have offended if I had not been drinking, been abused as a child, if my wife showed me more affection") and projection of responsibility (for example, "they wanted it," "they enjoyed it," "they came on to me"). These distorted beliefs are examined and challenged. The men work through their distortions to replace them with reality-based beliefs.

Men are also asked to examine the level of forethought, decision making, planning and grooming (a slow progression of manipulations used by some offenders to gain trust, to initiate physical contact and to ultimately gain sexual access) that goes into committing a sexual offence. Typically an individual's initial response to discussing the forethought involved in an offence is to indicate that "it just happened." As men become more comfortable and feel safer in treatment, with support and challenging, they are able to describe the extensive planning that precedes most offences. This process of disclosure promotes honesty, accountability and a recognition of the seriousness of their offending behaviour. Discussing the forethought and manipulation involved in offending also allows men to face and deal with the shame often attached to their knowledge of the premeditation and contemplation involved in their behaviour. Focusing on the planning element of the crime provides further clues for risk management strategies. For example, someone who volunteers to baby-sit as a means of gaining access to potential victims would need to commit to not placing himself in situations alone with children.

Someone who "cruises" to seek out a potential victim when angry would need to commit to not driving aimlessly, to avoid driving in certain locations (for example, if there was a particular area where they looked for victims) and to not drive when they are feeling angry.

Together, the Unhealthy Life Cycle (the emotional, cognitive and behavioural precursors) and the Crime Cycle (deviant sexual fantasy, cognitive distortions and planning) constitute an "Offence Cycle." Knowing and understanding one's Offence Cycle allows for insight into past offending and future risk factors, and provides direction as to the types of coping skills that need to be developed or further refined in order to avoid and/or manage an individual's particular risk factors.

Enhancing men's understanding of the harm caused by sexual-offending behaviour is another offence-specific treatment component. Men learn about the harm done not only to victim/survivors of sexual abuse/assault, but also to these people's families and friends, as well as to the larger community. The consequences and harm caused to the men themselves, as well as to their family, friends and community are also explored. In addressing harm done, men are not only supported in developing knowledge about the trauma associated with sexual victimization, but also in learning about and practising empathy development, particularly as it relates to their victim/survivors and the indirect victims of their offending.

Important lessons are also learned through exploring early life experiences. Men work on coming to understand how their families of origin and developmental experiences have shaped them. These insights are not developed as a source for blaming or to create a sense of self-pity. Rather, they are examined in order to help men understand other factors: where and how they have learned to manage emotions and why certain feelings are powerful triggers for them; where their attitudes, beliefs and perceptions were formulated; and why they may have adopted certain styles of coping. Attending and bringing resolution to childhood issues often helps the men come to terms with core emotions. This provides a strong foundation on which other treatment/healing gains can develop. Addressing these core issues is believed to be a critical component of long-term risk management.

Contemporary teachings focus directly on sexuality, both unhealthy and healthy. Treatment explores the messages men have received regarding sexuality and about themselves as sexual beings. This includes discussing early sexual experiences, exposure to and experience of sexual abuse, sexual experiences in relationships, the use of sex as a form of coping and sexual dysfunction. Pornography is also discussed, particularly related to the role of pornography in the development of attitudes toward females, perceptions about sexuality and its link to offending behaviour. As previously noted, treatment specifically attends to the men's inappropriate sexual interests, fantasies and arousal. In focusing on healthy sexuality, men explore healthy sexual attitudes and behaviours, positive attitudes towards women and relationships, communication and sexuality, and intimacy.

While this is by no means an exhaustive list of the teachings associated with the contemporary treatment portion of the blended approach, it does highlight some of the key areas.

Pipe carriers and Elders have brought many wonderful and important teachings to the treatment/healing process. While the teachings have varied depending on the spiritual helpers' own instruction and life experiences, the following represents some of the primary teachings delivered as part of the blended program.

Often men are provided with Medicine Wheel or Circle of Life Teachings. These teachings focus on the gifts and lessons associated with the "four directions" (north, south, east and west). For example, men are taught about the east, the spiritual dimension, where the eagle representing love and strength is found. They learn about the south, the location of the emotional domain and the home of the mouse, representing fear and truth. They are taught about the west, the physical dimension, where the bear representing healing and introspection is found. They also learn about the north, the location of the mental dimension and the home of the buffalo, representing wisdom. There are a number of other teachings that go along with these fundamental lessons about the four directions (some of these teachings are described by Bopp, Bopp, Brown, and Lane,1984).

Pipe carriers and Elders have identified other essential teachings. These have been referred to as "the four basic teachings" (the teachings of faith, honesty, kindness/caring and sharing) and "the seven sacred teachings" (the teachings of respect, honesty, love, truth, wisdom, humility and patience). Other teachings given to the men by the pipe carriers and Elders have included the importance of holism, trust, hope, a positive attitude and the need for forgiveness in one's life (Ellerby and Ellerby, 1998). In addition, Elders and pipe carriers teach about the importance of the spirit world. They also stress the importance of Mother Earth and use this to teach the men to understand who they are and how they fit in society. Another common teaching is about the importance of the "good road." Men are taught that they choose the path or the road they go down in life and that they know the difference between right and wrong. Elders and pipe carriers relate the need to be accountable to yourself, for your decisions, to others and to the Creator. While it is our belief that all of these teachings are relevant to the management of sexual-offending behaviour, some specific teachings related to sexual abuse are given. These include teachings around the inappropriateness of incest, the importance of respecting women and children and the importance of maintaining healthy relationships with people.

A blending of contemporary and traditional teachings comes in the form of the development of Wellness Plans. Wellness Plans outline a variety of coping strategies that can assist an individual to both avoid and manage their particular risk factors. This plan details both coping skills specific to offending (for example, high risk situations to avoid, ways of managing deviant sexual fantasies and arousal, challenges to offence-specific distortions) and more general but related strategies (for example, having healthy support people, talking about problems, maintaining a clean and sober lifestyle, self-care activities, developing healthy/pro-social relationships). In many instances Wellness Plans are organized along the four human dimensions. In these plans coping strategies particularly relevant to each domain are identified. For example, such a plan would consider the mental (monitoring self-talk, challenging distorted thoughts, considering consequences), the spiritual (prayer, smudging, counselling with Elder, participation in ceremonies), the emotional (paying attention to and identifying feelings, not holding emotions in, talking about feelings, not pretending things are okay and managing specific emotions such as anger) and the physical (attending to personal hygiene, getting proper sleep, healthy diet, exercise).

While there are certainly some differences between the contemporary and the traditional teachings, we have found them to be consistent in the messages being given and in the objectives of the teachings. Men in the program benefit from learning in two different ways and from receiving comprehensive and complementary teachings that reinforce each other.

The Continuum and Connectedness of Care

It has been important for us, and consistent with a holistic orientation, to attempt to develop a continuum of care that allows for continuity in the treatment/healing experience. We have been very fortunate to be able to deliver programming in, and develop connections between, the medium and minimum-security federal correctional institutions in Manitoba and link these to our community program. As a result, federally incarcerated men in Manitoba have the ability to work with the same team of helpers across sites and over the course of their sentence. While the types of treatment/healing services provided vary at each site, the clinical and traditional team and the treatment/healing philosophy and approach remains consistent.

For incarcerated men in our program, efforts are made to facilitate their participation in programming within the least restrictive environment. For example, men incarcerated in the medium-security institution may, after progress in programs at this site, be supported to continue their treatment/healing in the minimum-security institution. In many instances men from the minimum-security institution are prepared for release to the community by attending the blended group in the community, on passes from the institution. This enables individuals to become familiar with and comfortable in this group and to have this support in place prior to their release.

There has also been a link back to the institution for men in the community as sweat-lodge ceremonies have been conducted at the sacred grounds of the minimum-security institution. Men in the community have attended these ceremonies along with those individuals incarcerated at the institution. This shared community–institutional ceremony has provided an opportunity for the incarcerated men to heal alongside of those who have made the transition back to the community. They are able to hear what the transition is like, what obstacles may present themselves and how they might cope with issues that arise when they are released. It also serves to promote realistic expectations about their release. This is significant, as unrealistic and unmet expectations are a major contributing factor to men failing to maintain themselves in the community (Atkinson, Ellerby, Foss and Cota, 1991). The men attending the ceremony from the community describe feeling positive about supporting the men who are still incarcerated. They are also reminded of where they have come from and the need to be vigilant in the continuation of their growth.

Once men are established in the community, there is an effort to support and extend the continuum of care to their home communities. In this regard efforts are made to liaise with communities to support the men in the process of returning home and to provide the community with information that might help them accept their member back (for example, details about their member's treatment/healing experiences and gains, risk factors and wellness plans). The success of this process has varied greatly, largely depending on the level of acceptance, interest, stability and health of the home community. Some communities have actively participated in a process to support their member's return home, while others have not demonstrated an interest in such a process or have not wanted the offender to return home (Ellerby and Stonechild, 1998, LaPrairie, 1996).

Challenges Of A Blended Treatment/Healing Model

The development and implementation of this blended model has not come without difficulties. We have faced three main challenges that we continually attempt to resolve.

One of the challenges of providing the ceremonial component of the blended program in an institutional environment has been maintaining the focus on our particular client group. While the sweat-lodge ceremonies are specifically for the men in the blended sexual offender treatment/healing program, often other incarcerated men (who are not sexual offenders) attend the sacred grounds wishing to participate in the ceremony. Because of the spiritual nature of this ceremony we have struggled with how to address this issue. We have not wanted to place Elders in the position of telling men they cannot attend this particular sweat-lodge ceremony; however, we are also mindful that having diversity of offences among participants appears to affect the experience. When men who have not committed sexual offences attend, men in the blended program have expressed concerns about their safety as a result of the low status of, and animosity towards, sexual offenders in prison. As well, we have found that when the participants in the sweat-lodge are all men who have committed sexual offences, the level of openness, self-disclosure and emotional depth of the prayers and discussions is significantly greater. As a result, we have had to walk the fine balance of being respectful of some Elders' position of not excluding people from ceremonies while respecting the safety and needs of the men in our program.

Another difficulty we have encountered, both directly and indirectly, concerns the rarely publicized problems associated with inauthentic Elders and Elders with unhealthy behaviours. As the practice of traditional ways of healing becomes more prominent in corrections, individuals who claim to be Elders but who do not have the prerequisite skills, teachings or gifts apply for Elder positions. The process of hiring spiritual Elders has not been well-established or documented. In addition, checking qualifications and authenticity is often not an easy task. It is, however, imperative that there be more open dialogue about the hiring of Elders and that better ways of screening and authenticating credentials of individuals claiming to be spiritual Elders be developed.

Inauthentic or unhealthy Elders can cause significant damage to those under their care, leaving people feeling fear, mistrust, helplessness and anger (Ellerby and Bedard, 2000). The importance of having healthy Elders is significant as individuals in Elder positions at correctional institutions have a great deal of influence over the people they work with, many of whom are quite vulnerable. Conversely, there are some incarcerated individuals who are quite controlling and manipulative who can easily take advantage of and exploit an individual in an Elder position who is not really a Spiritual Elder or who is an Elder struggling with personal issues and behaviours. Therefore, it is important that these individuals be credible, skilled and gifted.

Intervening in cases where Elders are known to have engaged in inappropriate and potentially damaging behaviour is often difficult for both individuals and systems (for example, private and government agencies and institutions). Elders engaging in inappropriate conduct are often not held accountable for their behaviours for a range of reasons, some of which include: the status Elders enjoy, the fear people mistreated by an Elder experience, the mystique of their "gifts" and "powers," a lack of knowledge about spiritual practice as employed by Elders, the scarcity of organized formal regulatory bodies for Elders (for example, a council of Elders) and, at times, a system's concerns for the political ramifications of action against an Elder.

It has been noted that one way to facilitate more openness in acknowledging and addressing unhealthy behaviours by Elders is to stop placing them on a pedestal and recognize them as human beings who need to be accountable to the community for their conduct (Ellerby and Bedard, 2000). As a result of our experiences working with Elders, we inform individuals in this position that while we respect the gifts they bring to the program, they are equal members of the team and will be treated as such.

There is clearly a need for greater discussion about Elder accountability and a need for other traditional helpers, individuals, communities, agencies and institutions to become involved in a dialogue about how best to respond to these difficult situations. Ellerby (1999) provides an excellent guide for agencies and institutions employing Elders. He provides practical information and direction related to hiring Elders and identifies protocol to consider in working with spiritual healers.

The final challenge we have encountered has been gaining the interest, concern and support of the men's home communities. There is a significant stigma associated with having committed a sexual offence and there are communities who will shun members who have been involved in these types of behaviours (Ellerby and Stonechild, 1998; LaPrairie, 1996). Although it is understandable that communities may be fearful or may not want to deal with individuals who have caused harm in the community, there is a need for greater community education and community involvement. As a participant in a community circle eloquently related:

> We have to remember that for our relatives who are in the prisons and our relatives who have done things that have not been good for us or for them, that they are still our people. They still belong to us. We still have a responsibility for them and they have a responsibility to us. (in Ellerby and Bedard, 2000)

Benefits of a Blended Treatment/Healing Model

The development of the blended treatment/healing model has been an attempt to provide a more meaningful treatment experience for Aboriginal men who did not relate well to a cognitive-behavioural approach. In applying this blended model, we have seen Aboriginal men show an increased interest in participating in this stream of treatment and their feedback has been positive and supportive of this approach. The blended model has also received support from psychologists, therapists, Elders and pipe carriers. Helpers in this area have recognized and described the positive growth of men in the blended program and have noted their increased commitment to the treatment/healing process. Mental health professionals and healers have not only described the benefits of this approach, they have also identified the need for this type of intervention (Ellerby and Ellerby, 1998; Williams, Vallee and Staubi, 1997). Finally, the benefits of this model have been evident in the reduction in rates of treatment dropouts, terminations and suspensions and recidivism among the Aboriginal men in the blended program (Ellerby and Stonechild, 1998).

It has been our contention that if we develop and deliver programming that meets the needs of the individuals with whom we work, rather than attempting to fit them into our preconceived notion of a program, we are more likely to successfully reach them and facilitate change. This appears to be the case in the blended model. We have worked to combine the best of what we know about treatment and healing and have observed the rewards of this cooperative effort in the growth and wellness of the men in the program.

Notes

1. A cognitive-behavioural program focuses on cognitive intervention techniques and behavioural skill-training procedures to bring about change. The relapse prevention model for sexual offender treatment is adopted from the addictions field and is designed to support the maintenance of change over time. Individuals are taught to anticipate and cope with problems that have the potential to contribute to returning them to a behaviour they are trying to stop. In the case of sexual offenders, the program aims at preventing a re-offence.
2. A pipe carrier is given the responsibility of caring for the pipe, a sacred object of prayer. Typically an Elder will give the gift of the pipe to an individual worthy of this responsibility. Pipe carriers can then use this pipe in ceremonies for prayer and healing.

Chapter 6

The Ma Mawi Wi Chi Itata Stony Mountain Project:
Blending Contemporary and Traditional Approaches for Male Family Violence Offenders
Jocelyn Proulx and Sharon Perrault

> I don't want to keep explaining myself, that I came from prison, and been dysfunctional all my life, through different places and institutions. I don't want to keep blaming myself for what I do, I want to be responsible [for] what I act like and what I say.... I have a lot of feelings for her and I don't want it to end up in any kind of violence.

This chapter is dedicated to all men who are searching for alternatives to violence.

Family violence has historically been a well-kept secret among families and communities. It is only in recent years that policing of family violence and specialized court procedures have been developed. These have been joined by shelter and treatment programs for women and children and programs specifically designed for treating men's violence. The challenge faced by service providers in the field of family violence has become evident as we continue to ponder new initiatives and solutions towards ending the cycle of violence. Although government decision makers, policy-makers and practitioners have made much progress towards establishing new legislation, securing funding, and implementing programs to help families living with violence, much work still remains to be completed. Family violence does not exist in isolation, but rather manifests itself among a myriad of other issues such as addictions, incarceration and prostitution. Service provider agencies and institutions must work at addressing these issues directly within family violence programs, or as part of a larger initiative offering many programs to help individuals cope with, and heal from, family violence. Although the issues remain the same, the focus differs in programming for children, women and men. This chapter focuses on a program developed for incarcerated male family violence offenders. A blended programming model that incorporates both mainstream and Aboriginal elements is utilized and presented as an effective approach for healing from family violence. The Ma Mawi Wi Chi Itata Family Violence Program was developed out of a recognition of the institutional abuse that underlies the violence in Aboriginal communities combined with an understanding that family violence has similar characteristics across all communities.

Institutional Abuse of Aboriginal People

Colonization has left Aboriginal people, as a whole, exposed to racism, exploitation and institutionalized abuse. These violations have ranged from blatant to subtle and from personalized affronts to legal policy. Many Aboriginal people have encountered institutional abuse in foster homes, residential schools and prisons and through social policies such as the 60s swoop that removed children from their families. A significant proportion of Aboriginal children were removed from their families and educated and raised in residential schools, situated far from the reserves. Many were not allowed parental visitations. Within these institutions, they often experienced physical, sexual and psychological abuse, and neglect (York, 1990). Shame was associated with being Aboriginal: children had their hair cut, were separated from their siblings and were given new names (McGillivray, 1997). The schools were administrated by missionaries who promoted the Christian religion and forbade traditional spiritualism. Speaking Aboriginal languages was strongly discouraged; many children were punished for speaking their own language (Palmer and Cooke, 1996; Lee, 1992). English was taught and its use enforced. Aboriginal people and their traditions were viewed as barbaric and efforts were made to eradicate traditional ways and replace them with mainstream beliefs (McGillivray, 1997).

In the 1960s and 1970s, in accordance with prevailing child welfare policy, many Aboriginal children in Canada were removed from their homes (due to parental abuse, suspected abuse or perceived family dysfunction) and adopted into predominantly Caucasian urban homes. This became known as the "60s swoop." Large numbers of children were relocated to adoptive homes in the United States following an advertisement campaign in local newspapers (McGillivray, 1997; York, 1990). Going to Caucasian, middle-class, urban homes from Aboriginal reserves, these children suffered the loss of their culture; many lost both culture and country. In most cases, Caucasian adoptive parents did nothing to learn about the Aboriginal traditions, and were unprepared to help these children explore their Aboriginal culture or to cope with the racism they faced in a Caucasian environment (York, 1990).

In Canada, there is an overrepresentation of Aboriginal children in the child welfare system (Palmer and Cooke, 1996; Zylberberg, 1991). Although many foster homes offer care and comfort to children, some are characterized by abuse, neglect and racism (McFadden and Ryan, 1991; Palmer and Cooke, 1996). Children placed in institutional care, such as group homes or youth care facilities, also face potential abuse from staff and other children (Tomkiewicz, 1984). Individuals who have been removed from their families may find themselves in foster families that are equally, or more, dangerous. Numerous consecutive foster placements are common (Gil, 1982), and, along with poor family functioning and abuse, are significantly related to chronic delinquency in children aged 11 to 18 years (Towberman, 1994). This pattern may escalate into violence and criminal behaviour which often leads to youth and adult incarceration in environments that are equally susceptible to abuse and violence.

Removal from families and placement in foreign, punitive and racist environments, interferes with healthy identity development (Shkilnyk, 1985; York, 1990; Zylberberg, 1991). It also hinders the process of bonding with caregivers, and, in Aboriginal children, increases feelings of isolation and alienation from family and culture (Lee, 1992). These experiences engender feelings of fear, anger and helplessness. Many run away from these situations to equally destructive ones or further institutional placements (Palmer and Cooke, 1996). Most children who experienced residential schooling, foster care and other institutional care incurred damage to their physical, behavioural, affective, cognitive and social development that has had long-lasting effects. Reduced opportunities for secure attachments result in problems relating to, caring for and trusting others (Hirschbach, 1982). The loss of positive parenting models adversely affects development of parenting skills, leaving subsequent generation of children vulnerable to child welfare placements (Lee, 1992; Palmer and Cooke, 1996).

Although many of the institutional abuses experienced by Aboriginal people have ended, a cycle of violence within Aboriginal communities has developed. Spousal abuse in Aboriginal families is approximately seven times the national average and the incidence of sexual abuse is very high (Timpson, 1995). Many men who commit family violence have an extensive history of violence in their own lives (Pagelow, 1981; MacEwan, 1994). In general, the greater the severity of the abuse experienced, the stronger the relationship to family violence offending in later life (Milner, Robertson, and Rogers, 1990).

In accordance with social learning theory (Bandura, 1973), individuals experiencing multiple forms and levels of abuse have learned to interact in violent ways. Witnessing violence between parents and other family members teaches individuals to expect violence within the context of love, affection and intimate relationships. As adults, their violence increases the risk that their children will be placed in institutional care and, for men in particular, that they will be incarcerated. A large proportion of incarcerated men have experienced childhood victimization in the form of sexual abuse, physical abuse and/or neglect (Dutton and Hart, 1992; 1994; Weeks and Widom, 1998). Thus the abuse incurred by Aboriginal people through Canadian social policy is perpetuated through multiple generations.

Childhood Abuse and Family Violence Offenders

Victims of childhood abuse and batterers display similar cognitive, emotional and behavioural patterns. Among these is dissociative symptoms (Alexander and Anderson, 1997; Chu and Dill, 1990; Briere, 1992; Sanders and Giolas, 1991). Many sex offenders with a history of childhood sexual abuse have not disclosed their own abuse and experience greater difficulty talking about their own childhood abuse than about their sexual offences. Dissociation of the self from the abuse experience helps to protect them from confronting the emotions associated with the abuse and serves to maintain the anger that fuels their sexual offences. Feelings of power and control experienced while committing the abuse reinforces the offence and alleviates the feelings of vulnerability and powerlessness that are characteristic of male sexual abuse victims (Freeman-Longo, 1986). The dissociation from their own abuse also allows them to separate themselves from the suffering of their victims: they do not associate their own abuse-related pain and trauma with the trauma they inflict on their victims. Some focus only on what they see as the benefits or positive aspects of their offence, such as affection for the child. Many begin treatment with no concept of the harm they have done to their victims (Freeman-Longo, 1986).

In addition, interpersonal relationships are affected by abuse. Abused children and batterers tend to form insecure attachments, become isolated, develop feelings of shame (Berk, 1997; Browne and Finkelhor, 1986; Dutton and Golant, 1995; Dutton and Holtzworth-Munroe, 1997; Hofford, 1991), display deficits in dyadic relationship functioning, and experience lower satisfaction with intimate relationships (Hunter, 1991; Meston, 1993; Young, Bergandi, and Titus, 1994). Low self-esteem, identity confusion and poor ego strength are common correlates of childhood abuse and perpetration of family violence (Hunter, 1991; Milner, 1988; Rogers and Terry, 1984; Steele, 1987).

Another effect of victimization is a pervasive sense of loss of control over the environment as well as over one's self and one's body. This leads many victims to attempt to regain control; perpetration of violence is one means of exerting and displaying control. (This issue is of particular concern for men, since their socialization emphasizes control as part of the male gender role.) Aggressive behaviour intimidates others and makes them compliant and conciliatory. The links between domestic abuse by males and feelings of powerlessness, a low tolerance for being controlled and a sense of control being external to the self have been well documented (Ellis and Milner, 1981; Petric, Olson, and Subotnik, 1994).

For many men, this violence has brought them into the correctional system. Within the correctional facilities men face further abuse and violence; aggressive behaviour and interpersonal isolation are often mandatory for survival within the prisons. Thus the violent behaviour that brought them into the institution is reinforced and perpetuated. Few have the chance to implement anger management or social interaction training techniques. With few new skills learned, and the constant reinforcement of aggression and violence, inmates have limited opportunities to change their lives upon release. Their violence continues, often reintroducing them into the correctional system. Therefore, for some men, violence has been a consistent component within their lives from a very early age. This consistency makes violence both an expected and normative event, and a habitual aspect of their interpersonal relationships.

The Cycle of Violence

The typical cycle of violence has periods of escalation preceding an episode of violence, followed by stages of regret, remorse, self-berating verbalizations and conciliation. The remorse may indicate a sense of dissatisfaction with this behaviour, or at least with the results of the behaviour. It may also feed into an existing sense of low self-esteem. However, the pattern has been well-ingrained into the repertoire of family interaction. Extinguishing these abusive behaviours is insufficient for behaviour change; alternative forms of communication need to be introduced and learned.

Intergenerational abuse is evident in many Aboriginal families and is reflected in the Aboriginal men incarcerated in correctional facilities throughout Canada. The historic experience of colonization has contributed to a damaged sense of identity and self-worth, and a loss of language, culture and community for many Aboriginal people. This history contributes to and exacerbates the occurrence of intergenerational violence. For Aboriginal people, their shared experience as a nation cannot be separated from the abuse they experience or perpetrate. This common historical link to abuse and violence creates a need for culturally appropriate programming that will acknowledge and incorporate these experiences into both the content and the process of therapy.

The Need for Aboriginal-Specific Programming

Social support, acquiring knowledge and skills, and counselling are all essential in the process of healing from abusive experiences. The literature suggests that childhood social support acts as a mediator between the experience of violence during childhood, and subsequent perpetration of violence in adulthood (Calisco and Milner, 1994). Social isolation and a lack of peer and familial support are common in abusive parents (Milner and Chilamkurti, 1991). Social support provides a sense of community and care and encourages individuals to persevere with treatment and therapy.

Because family violence results from learned behaviours, knowledge and learning are necessary components of the healing process. Helping people understand the reasons for their violent actions, as well as suggesting other more adaptive responses, helps them develop an objective perspective on their actions and facilitates behavioural change. Counselling provides a structured form of support and allows the exploration and confrontation of emotions and issues within a safe and confidential environment in which trust can be built and feelings and ideas verbalized. Left unexpressed, these cognitions and emotions could lead to the perpetuation of violent behaviour. Alternative techniques and strategies for dealing with these feelings are encouraged and supported by the counsellor and others (in group therapy).

The effectiveness of these components of family violence programming are maximized when presented through culturally sensitive mechanisms. Aboriginal-specific programming is directly relevant to the lives and experiences of Aboriginal people and is important in programming for Aboriginal offenders (Waldram and Wong, 1995). Groups of people with similar experiences and cultural backgrounds may reduce intragroup conflict and increase cohesiveness and supportive attitudes. An atmosphere of acceptance and understanding is more easily generated when all individuals in the group have shared a similar history and experience, and there is respect for that history within the program and by its facilitators. Information that is presented in terms and methods that are not only respectful of, but directly incorporate the norms, traditions and ceremonies of Aboriginal culture has the potential to increase the program's success rate.

Family violence offenders, particularly those who are extremely violent, often drop out of therapy or treatment (Wolfe, Edwards, Manion, and Koverola, 1988). Culturally specific programming may increase the acceptance of and participation in programs. Greater personal relevance such as that provided by the spiritual aspects of an Aboriginal program, may also increase long-term effects as they become incorporated in daily life (Waldram and Wong, 1995). A return to the traditional teachings and beliefs may renew or instill a sense of identity, thereby increasing self-worth and self-efficacy. Waldram (1993) found that incarcerated Aboriginal offenders had very positive attitudes towards spiritual programs implemented to increase knowledge of culture and healing. Many felt that these programs allowed them to resolve identity conflicts and provide them with a means of coping with their incarceration. Cultural relevance, then, might contribute to the success of family violence programs by encouraging perseverance even when program content is difficult or distressing, and by building confidence in new conflict resolution and relationship skills.

A significant component of culturally relevant programming is the use of Aboriginal facilitators and Elders who can more credibly present Aboriginal teachings. When group members can identify culturally with their facilitators, feelings of closeness, confidence and trust develop, and the members are enabled to confront and deal with their violence. The understanding and respect of Aboriginal facilitators leads to the validation of group members and their experiences. Thus their self-esteem improves, as does their trust in others—two features essential to successful treatment and healing.

Much of mainstream programming in the area of family violence is based on well-documented theory and research: methods and content have been established as theoretically sound and effective. The blending of effective mainstream programs and Aboriginal-specific program aspects is one means of providing quality family violence programs to the Aboriginal community (Waldram and Wong, 1995). The content is determined by mainstream theories; the process is based on Aboriginal traditions and life experiences. Direct references to colonization and its impact on attachment and trust development may be incorporated into program content. Thus the best aspects of both mainstream and Aboriginal approaches are utilized for maximum effectiveness within the Aboriginal community. Blended programs of this type are currently being more widely applied. The Ma Mawi Wi Chi Itata Family Violence community-based services and the program delivered at Stony Mountain Correctional Facility exemplify this type of blended programming.

The Ma Mawi Wi Chi Itata Family Violence Program— Stony Mountain Project

The Ma Mawi Wi Chi Itata Family Violence Program has operated in Winnipeg since 1987. The program began with services available to women and children and then expanded to include programming for men. Many of the men who attend the community-based program have been referred through Parole and Probation Services. In 1993, the Family Violence Program contracted with Correctional Service Canada to deliver the program to Aboriginal inmates at Stony Mountain Federal Correctional Facility. Given that approximately 49 percent of the federally incarcerated inmates in Manitoba are Aboriginal (Griffiths and Verdun-Jones, 1994), and the majority of them are either incarcerated for violent offences or have a history of violent behaviour with their partners, the need for family violence programming within correctional institutions such as Stony Mountain is clear.

The Stony Mountain Family Violence Program offers a combination of mainstream and traditional teachings as well as a combination of closed group sessions, and individual and Elder counselling. The goals include the reduction of violence in the Aboriginal community, healing from past abuse and violence, and the creation of physically and emotionally healthy Aboriginal families. The main objectives of the Stony Mountain Family Violence Program are to have men accept full responsibility for their violent behaviours and to teach them the skills that will help them eliminate violence from their intimate and family relationships. The opportunity for the men to be exposed to teachings and practices which help them develop a positive cultural identity is an integral part of the program.

Towards these ends, the men are provided with a setting in which they feel safe to disclose their personal stories related to the violence they have perpetrated. The group provides a safe environment where batterers can decrease their sense of isolation and dependency on the victim. Establishing a peer support system and developing interpersonal skills allows the men to meet their own needs in a constructive manner. Within the group the men are expected to follow rules of mutual respect, non-violence and dedication to healing.

Alternative means of dealing with feelings of anger and with the various other effects of violence are taught. Negative behaviour patterns exhibited with family, fellow inmates, and institutional authority are targeted for change. Practising new skills increases the likelihood that these abilities will become a common component of the men's behavioural repertoire. Using more effective communication skills (such as listening to their partners and articulating their own feelings) and conflict management skills (such as making assertive statements and learning to compromise) will ultimately enhance their lives, the lives of their family members and their interactions within the institution.

The healing process that the men experience while attending the Stony Mountain Family Violence Program helps them look at their childhood experiences within their family of origin. Many report feelings of having lost their childhood as a result of growing up in violent homes. Through sharing personal experiences the men are better able to resolve feelings of ambivalence concerning their childhood. They begin to understand and integrate the experiences of childhood violence with their violent behaviour as adults. With the process of education and the practice of specific skills, perpetrators of violence can unlearn the violence to which they have been socialized. For example, many people turn to various forms of compulsive coping behaviours such as substance abuse as a means of dealing with their issues of abuse, personal pain and negative self-image. These associations must be identified and understood by the men before they can completely heal.

As part of bringing individuals back to their culture and enhancing cultural identity, the facilitators and the Elder directly teach Aboriginal history, traditional ways and ceremonies. These are all essential to building a cultural identity and pride in that identity. A complete sense of identity requires acceptance and incorporation of all the aspects of self. For many Aboriginal men a security and pride in their culture has been curtailed by violence, racism and various other abuses. The program seeks to renew security and pride in the Aboriginal identity. Issues of colonization and racism are explored and a sense of respect for Aboriginal culture and traditions is imparted through the facilitators' and Elders' direct teachings and through their behaviour towards each other. Participation in ceremonies and exposure to culturallybased stories help establish a sense of cultural identity which can be incorporated into a system of beliefs.

Several issues are addressed in the closed men's group program. The topics presented follow the model of the medicine wheel. Each direction represents a different task or focus. The eastern direction represents truthfulness and new beginnings. Some of the topics covered in this section are the cycle of violence, dealing with emotions, socialization and discussion of the men's most violent incident. The southern direction represents the ability to express negative emotions and emotional growth. Among the topics covered are family of origin, shame and guilt, psychological abuse, colonization and stereotypes, and culture and self-esteem. The western direction represents commitment to the path of personal development and power. The topics discussed include the impact of violence on children, parenting, assertiveness, relationships and jealousy, and sexuality. The northern direction represents the capacity to dwell in the centre of things, and healing. This section includes a woman sharing her story of abuse, sharing circles, and revisiting goals and achievements. A sweat-lodge ceremony concludes each section. The end of the group is marked by a feast and graduation ceremony.

Throughout the program, information is contextualized within the Aboriginal experience. For example, discussions of family of origin, parenting and sexual abuse present general information as well as information specifically relevant to Aboriginal people. Wherever possible, research pertaining to Aboriginal people is introduced. Topics such as colonization and its effects provide a basis for recognition of a shared history. Through these means, group participants share common experiences related to culture, family and community. Several ceremonies are introduced including the pipe ceremony, the smudge ceremony, and sharing and talking circles. An Elder presides over all the ceremonies and teaches participants about these ceremonies and traditions. It is believed that effective family violence programming must reflect the cultural values of Aboriginal people. Programs will only be accepted and well-attended by the Aboriginal population when they can identify with the program philosophy and ideology.

The Family Violence Program affords participants many opportunities to practise identifying the physical and emotional cues that precede a violent episode. Learning through practice and repetition reinforces utilizing alternatives to violence when confronted with potential situations for reacting aggressively. In addition, cultural teachings and traditions, inherent in the program, encourage participants to live a violence-free lifestyle. Reparation of their self-esteem and identity is possible as they become further entrenched in and familiar with their culture. Elders and spiritual teachers can lead the way through exemplification of positive role models. They are able to intensify the essence and meaning of healing the mind, body and spirit. Eventually, the men begin to realize that violence towards their family and community members leads to the erosion of the very healing they are seeking.

The format of the Stony Mountain Project differs slightly from the community-based program. The community-based program has eighteen sessions, whereas the Stony Mountain Project has thirty-seven sessions. Some of the family violence issues are addressed in the open groups for the men of the community. Open groups are flexible and can be accessed as needed, therefore group composition fluctuates from session to session. Closed groups are structured and contain a small number of the same participants from beginning to end. Inmates do not have the opportunity for open group preliminary work, thus all issues must be discussed in the closed group. Although essential issues remain the same, the focus and activities are oriented either towards an institutional experience or a non-institutional experience. Men in both the community- and prison-based programs have had experience with violent lifestyles and have learned to integrate their violent attitudes and values to patterns of thinking and behaviour. Problems involving the legal system are experienced by both inmates and men from the community program.

The main difference between the two populations is that participants in the prison-based program tend to represent the more severe end of the violence spectrum.

Community Reintegration

This program is part of the federal and community effort to rehabilitate and reform the offender. Recently there have been discussions about the reintegration of the offender into community living and the rebuilding of inmates' family relationships. Preparation of the inmate for release and the reduction of his recidivism necessitate a careful examination of the needs of both the inmate and the community. It would be unrealistic to believe that all of the needs of the inmate and his family can be met within the confines of a correctional institution. Some responsibility for the inmate's reform and social and familial reintegration belongs to the community. Therefore, an ideal family violence program would include a collaborative approach between Correctional Service Canada and the community. Healing is an ongoing process that requires continued effort after release from prison (Waldram, 1993). This is the type of programming that has been introduced to the inmates at Stony Mountain.

Because there is a community-based program that is comparative to the program delivered within Stony Mountain, inmates have a familiar and responsive resource to access upon release. Inmates are more likely to seek out assistance from a familiar source. At the community-based program they will encounter some of the individuals they met in the institution. The program process will also be familiar. Open and closed groups, and individual counselling by Elders are available at the community level, allowing the men to tailor programming to their needs. The familiarity and flexibility of the program affords these men maximum opportunity for continued healing and living a violence-free life. Community-based programs provide the opportunity for the care and maintenance which the healing process requires.

Further, the community-based program offers men the opportunity to bring their partners and children for counselling. The Ma Mawi Wi Chi Itata Family Violence Program takes a holistic approach to programming. This holistic approach is respectful of the importance of families within the Aboriginal community. It is recognized that family violence victims and offenders do not exist in isolation but form an interactive unit, the dynamics of which are significant to the occurrence and cessation of violence. These families are also part of the larger Aboriginal community which can provide them with cultural teachings and support. Provision of treatment for the whole family can extend into family and couples therapy at other community agencies. The sense of family and community support received by men when their whole family is able to attend family violence counselling programs will serve to encourage them to maintain their path of healing and remain non-violent.

Evaluation of the Stony Mountain Project

An evaluation of the Family Violence Program Stony Mountain Project was completed in 1996 by the authors. Interviews were conducted with forty-six inmates who were past program participants, sixteen current program participants, ten case management officers and six guards. All interviewers were Aboriginal, as it was suggested by program facilitators that Aboriginal inmates would be more receptive to speaking with Aboriginal people. Some of the interviewers spoke Aboriginal languages, facilitating interviews with inmates who spoke English as a second language. Interviewers were trained in techniques such as rephrasing questions, probing and use of recording equipment. Providing information about institutional guidelines, including the use of appropriate caution when interacting with inmates and restrictions on items allowed in or out of the institution, was part of the training process. Informed consent was obtained and confidentiality assured. Protocols involved both closed- and open-ended questions. Responses to open-ended questions were tape recorded; responses to closed-ended questions were recorded on the protocol itself.

Results indicated that most (63 percent) of the men who participated in the program were motivated by a desire to learn more about themselves and their violence, and to find alternative means of dealing with their anger. Some respondents commented:

> *I want to learn not to be violent and want to find myself, get in touch with my feelings.*
>
> *I wanted to learn some reasons why I use violence and some ways to deal with it.*

Others (31 percent) were mandated to the program by their case management officer. One respondent said:

> *Actually, my case manager pointed it out to me, so I chose to go. I didn't realize I had a problem until I finished the program.*

Many inmates felt that the program had met their expectations, thus satisfaction with the program was extremely high (an average response of 6.33 on a scale of 1 to 7 where 1 is not at all satisfied and 7 is extremely satisfied). They stated,

> *Actually, they met more than my expectations.... I was surprised how the program was all together, especially in an institution like this. They had the circle and they bring in all the special secret ceremonies, grasses and spices.... The sweats, I never felt I would be involved in that, to me that was new.... It was a good experience for me. I really enjoyed it and I felt really at ease, comfortable with the people who were running the program, and the sweats and everything. I feel kind of connected to the program because they are so open and easy to talk to.*

The cultural components of the program, particularly the sweatlodge and smudge ceremonies, brought the greatest degree of satisfaction. Some men commented:

> *It is a place to heal (the sweat), a place to leave your anger, bad thoughts and bad things that have happened, to leave with the grandfathers. It also gave me a sense of direction, purpose.*

> *Every time they had a smudge I always prayed ... it makes me feel good.*

> *The eagle feather is like teachers, it is teaching. It is there to help you. A second little spirit. Whenever someone passes me an eagle feather, I am honoured.... The eagle feather represents honesty and truth.*

Inmates stated that some of the material and assignments was emotionally straining and unpleasant. Some of the most difficult tasks included:

> *Sharing my most violent incident.*

> *When it was my turn to speak because I was shy.*

A desire for a more lengthy program to allow more detailed information, and more practice and processing time was voiced.

An essential characteristic of the program is the participant/facilitator relationship. Inmates were most appreciative of facilitators' honesty, openness, trustworthiness and understanding, noting these characteristics:

> *Sense of humour, generous, understanding, caring, respected us as individuals.*
>
> *They talked with us on our level, easy to relate to. I think they are very open and took a committed, honest approach.*

For some inmates it was important that the facilitators be Aboriginal, as they felt it engendered trust and a degree of comfort:

> *They know how it is to an Aboriginal going through this violence. They can put themselves in our shoes.*

Even more important was the fact that facilitators came from the community rather than the institution. Participants felt that facilitators from outside of the institution were more likely to remain objective, and to maintain confidentiality of information imparted within the group:

> *That is probably why the group opened up so much ... because they were from the outside. If it was staff it would never happen.*

The prevalent belief was that facilitators from the institution would lack sensitivity and understanding towards inmates and their experiences, and would not maintain the trust necessary for disclosure of personal information. Two inmates voices these fears:

> *I think that is better than having to deal with the main staff in here because there [are] too many ... they tend to hold power here over you. So, if something goes wrong and they hold it against you, they hold a grudge in one way or another. It might fall back into the program like this.... There is no trust with the institutional staff.*
>
> *I wouldn't feel comfortable. I would feel that they were being a spy because they are working for the institution.... They are not really*

> *in to help us, they are there because it is their job. [They] must have some independence from the institution. [It is] very important that they stay separate.*

This fear persisted even with institutional staff facilitators who were Aboriginals:

> *It is still staff regardless if they are Aboriginal. The program will not run as well. Nobody is going to open up.*

A further advantage of having facilitators from an outside agency was the provision of a contact source and continued treatment upon release. One man commented:

> *Nice to know that somebody out in the community would go to the trouble of coming into a federal pen two or three times a week in order to help out the people in there and to offer a program that the pen can't offer, or won't offer. Community support, you know there are people out there that will help you.*

Overall, the ideal for inmates was to have non-institutional, community-based, Aboriginal facilitators. These are all features that characterize the current program.

Another part of the evaluation assessed the impact of the Family Violence Program on participants' behaviour, cognitions and emotions, from the perspective of the participants, case management officers and guards. Participants indicated that the program helped them to understand and control their violence and encouraged consideration of other people:

> *It helped with violence because a lot of times you run off the top with guys and girlfriends. I took a look at myself and where that anger is going to lead to and the consequences. The consequences basically, what they taught me, is something I never looked at before because I didn't care.... Feeling better about myself, and that is part of the not using violence or anger to get myself in trouble.*

> *It helped me learn where I went wrong.... To be able to communicate with your partner, your kids, your friends.*

> *It changed the way I thought about things and reacted.*

Most found opportunities to utilize the information they had learned in their interactions within the institution, helping them communicate and deal with emotions more effectively:

> *With my daily life in here with other inmates and staff, I have been able to implement it.*

> *On the phone I noticed that I could have yelled and screamed but I just kept my head.*

> *I talked to a friend of mine, and I tried to remind him about what he had learned in his relationship. I kinda pointed that out to him. It helped him and it helped me too.*

Case officers reported a moderate amount of change in inmates' behaviour towards others in the institution: an average score of 4.40 on a scale ranging from 1, indicating no change at all, to 7, indicating many changes. This observed change included an increased understanding of violence and its impact on others and a tendency to find alternative solutions to problems. Two inmates commented on the changes they observed:

> *A little more openness. More relaxed in their ability to communicate about some of their feelings regarding their culture. More self-aware, quieter, more at peace.... Family members have told us there is some change.*

> *We started off with an inmate who was anti-social but didn't wish to participate or do anything, but once we got him involved in the program, just at the spirituality side, it was just amazing, the change in him. Overall attitude, he adopted a lot of things he learned in the program and actually used it in the institution.*

Thus, there were reports of improved relationships and interactions between inmates and institutional staff. Guards who had more contact with the men noticed more change than did case management officers, who did not have daily contact with inmates. In general, guards and case officer providers felt that a program with Aboriginal-specific content was of great benefit to inmates and a much-needed service in Stony Mountain Federal Institution.

At the time of the evaluation, a voluntary post-program group provided continued counselling for the men. This group was expected to reinforce the information and techniques learned in the program and provide inmates with the social support required to implement change in their lives. This open group met once every two weeks; the agenda was set by the group at the beginning of each meeting. Four individuals from this group of six were interviewed. All found it satisfactory, stating that the group helped them to increase their knowledge and retain facilitator support. Unfortunately this follow-up group has since been discontinued due to poor attendance. The scheduling conflict between the group and other programs and employment made regular attendance difficult.

Thus, it can be concluded that there is both a need and a desire for an Aboriginal-specific family violence program within Stony Mountain Federal Correctional Facility. The need is defined by the number of Aboriginal inmates in the institution with a history of violent offences against partners and family members. The desire was clearly voiced by inmates and staff alike.

In addition, it appears to be important that this type of program be administered by an agency outside of the institution. A community agency is essential in fostering trust and providing the opportunity for continued counselling and treatment upon release. The trust generated by community facilitators instills a sense of confidentiality and respect that encourages disclosures and the sharing of sensitive information necessary to successful family violence programming. The familiarity of the men with the facilitators and the program itself will encourage them to access the community-based program upon leaving the institution. It may also encourage them to bring their partners and/or families for counselling and to allow themselves and their families to continue on a path of healing.

Expansion of the Stony Mountain Family Violence Program

Continuous efforts have been made to improve the program since its inception at Stony Mountain. For example, after the men indicated that the time allotted to consideration of their most violent incident was insufficient for complete exploration and resolution, this one session was expanded to three sessions. Facilitators and inmates have expressed greater satisfaction with this revision.

Currently an expansion of the program at Stony Mountain is underway. The one parenting session is being modified and two additional parenting sessions are being structured. These sessions cover the topics of normal child development, the effects of abuse on child development, discipline and responsible parenting. Further, three new sessions discussing sexual abuse, its effects, its relationship to violence and its relevance to the Aboriginal community will be added. Presently, inmates' experiences of sexual abuse have no designated place for discussion, yet many have disclosed incidents of child sexual abuse, and the literature has demonstrated that sexual abuse is associated with the development of violent behaviour and criminal involvement. The important effects of residential schooling and institutional care on parenting, abuse and violence will also be covered in subsequent sessions. Individual counselling on these new issues will be made available. Evaluations of the new sessions will be conducted, allowing for modifications and improved service with the continued goal of effective programming.

Recently, Correctional Service Canada has initiated a process of program accreditation. The goal is to establish reputable programs and utilize them throughout all federal correctional facilities. This process requires well-documented, effective programs. Part of the objective is to respond to the needs of Aboriginal inmates by providing Aboriginal-specific programming. It is the plan of the Ma Mawi Wi Chi Itata Family Violence Program to revise the current program into a high-intensity program, encompassing approximately seventy sessions, which will provide more detailed information and allow inmates a greater opportunity to practise and enhance various communication, anger-management and conflict-resolution skills. This high-intensity program will be recommended for inmates with a long-term sentence, and a long history of violence, and who require much time and/or practice at violence prevention and management skills. A moderate-intensity version similar to the one presently delivered would also be made available. This program will be recommended for inmates who have some violence issues, are not in the system or a particular facility for an extended period of time, and/or may have the ability to quickly grasp details and complex concepts. These programs will undergo evaluation and modification in order to create a program that is efficient, effective and comprehensive. The two program versions will be consistent in the manner in which family violence issues are addressed, and diverse enough to meet the needs of the men. Both will be submitted for accreditation, thereby providing quality Aboriginal-specific programming across Canada and meeting the needs of other incarcerated Aboriginal men.

Conclusion

Historically, within Aboriginal communities every family member had a role to play towards living a balanced, healthy lifestyle. Elders and leaders were chosen by their respective communities and the well-being of every community member was considered when prioritizing decisions affecting the community as a whole. Roles and responsibilities were articulated through the caregiving of immediate and extended family members. However, this intricate balance was affected by European contact. The enforcement of assimilation policies and procedures negated norms and values of Aboriginal life. Furthermore, it eroded the social and cultural fabric to which Aboriginal communities had adhered for centuries.

It has remained a continuing challenge for Aboriginal people to have available to them programming which reflects their needs and cultural experiences. Moreover, blending of contemporary and traditional programming requires careful consideration to maintain the integrity of the context and the cultural aspects. Individuals involved in the production and delivery of such programs need to be vigilant that participants' cultural and treatment needs are being met. Provision of blended programming is a learning experience for program planners, facilitators and participants. Often programs must be modified to better meet the needs of participants or to keep pace with changing times, circumstances and needs. Although little research on the structure and effectiveness of blended programming for Aboriginal people is available, this should change as more programs are initiated. Therefore many Aboriginal communities can learn from each other and benefit from various programming and implementation strategies. Aboriginal participants and communities will continue to gain confidence in the value of their own wisdom, traditions, and system of teaching and learning, and acquire a sense of control over what they teach others. The attainment of these goals will serve to encourage the exploration and expansion of culturally relevant programming and literature.

A revitalization of culturally specific healing and treatment methods continues to emerge in many Aboriginal communities across Canada. Diversions from the mainstream justice system are being established and new opportunities are being presented that better reflect the Aboriginal experience. By offering a diversity of Aboriginal-specific programming in communities and penal institutions, Aboriginal practitioners become better prepared to meet the daily challenges of working within family violence service provision.

There is no easy panacea for helping and teaching each other to live violence-free lifestyles. However, through diligent work and action-oriented research more effective family violence programming will continue to be born and nurtured. Many community-based practitioners realize the positive effects of research and evaluation, particularly when it is contextualized in a community-based framework that can enhance programming. Ultimately program participants and community members guide the movement towards effective programming. Research then both verifies and improves program content.

Aboriginal communities are now raising a clearer voice in identifying and addressing the needs of their people. This clarity has come from attending to and respecting the stated needs of offenders and victims in seeking guidance and healing. These communities have entered a new millennium with a shared vision and worldview, one in which every member within a community has an equal voice and a responsibility to share in the caretaking of one another. In so doing, there will eventually be a movement towards a milieu where mutual respect and nonviolence become the norm.

Finally, we must acknowledge the Creator and the legacy that has been given to Aboriginal people. Teachings that include kindness, respect, faith, sharing and caring leave no place for violence. When individuals challenge each other to live a violence-free lifestyle they honour that legacy, and opportunities become available for future generations to replicate these teachings. Through adopting various modalities of healing, Aboriginal people are able to repair the harm and reverse the impact of myriads of intergenerational acts of violence and abuse.

Conclusion

Sharon Perrault and Jocelyn Proulx

Aboriginal communities experience a high rate of family violence as indicated directly by the research presented in Chapters 2 and 3, and in the literature reviewed throughout this book. Current systems of response to this violence inadequately meet the needs of these communities, especially northern rural communities. As outlined in Chapters 2, 3 and 4, fear of and dissatisfaction with the systems and authorities who deal with family violence issues are commonly voiced by Aboriginals: women from northern communities in Manitoba reported that a fear of court proceedings would sometimes prevent them from reporting incidences of abuse; abused women in Winnipeg shelters indicated fears of not being believed, or of being blamed when reporting abuse. This experience of racism and lack of response sometimes kept women from notifying authorities about domestic violence. The research done with Aboriginal women, presented in Chapter 2, underlines the necessity not only to include counselling and community involvement in programming for offenders, but also to provide traditional healing in an atmosphere of cultural sensitivity. It was felt that violence in Aboriginal communities needed to be understood historically as a result of the violence and racism inflicted on Aboriginal people during colonization. Treatment should include components which would strengthen a positive cultural identity and promote harmony of the individual with the community through the use of traditional teachings.

With this understanding and awareness of the dimensions of the problem of violence Aboriginal communities have been formulating alternatives to mainstream programming. Diversion projects such as the Aboriginal Ganootamaage Justice Services of Winnipeg offer

Conclusion

Aboriginal offenders who have committed non-violent crimes the opportunity to complete a healing plan involving cultural ceremonies, self-discovery through talks with Elders and interactions with a community council and the victim. The goal is reconciliation, restitution and restoration of peaceful relations between the offender and the victim, so that the offender is healed by, and remains a part of the community.

The Native Clan Organizations Forensic Behavioral Management Clinic in Winnipeg has structured an alternative to their mainstream cognitive behavioural program for sex offenders. The program for Aboriginal sex offenders offers a more holistic approach that combines spirituality, traditional teachings and ceremonies with contemporary methods. Men with committed relationships are encouraged to bring partners for couples counselling. The program is provided within the community and within federal correctional facilities. Community participants attend some ceremonies within the institution and low-risk inmates are given day passes to attend sessions within the community. This provides inmates with a connection to the community upon release and supports the role of the community in helping to heal individuals from the effects of violence.

The Ma Mawi Wi Chi Itata Family Violence Program blends mainstream content with Aboriginal-specific processes. Programs are offered to children, women and men of the community and to inmates of Stony Mountain Federal Correctional Facility. Knowledge and skills related to ending family violence are combined with Aboriginal teachings, ceremonies and presentations on the impact of colonization. A holistic perspective on the origins, effects, and means of healing from family violence is presented. Individual counselling is available to men, women and children to help them heal and lead violence-free lives. The community programs facilitate community reintegration and support of healing for Aboriginal inmates released from Stony Mountain Federal Correctional Facility.

Although the research and alternative programs presented have revealed valuable information and suggested effective means of dealing with violence and crime, they have also indicated some areas where further work and research are needed to improve the successful use of Aboriginal-specific programming. In general the predisposition on the part of Aboriginals to mistrust community leaders and helping professionals was problematic.

Thomlinson, Erickson and Cook, in Chapter 2, found this mistrust to be a major impediment to successful alternative programming. This mistrust related to the belief that these individuals had not dealt with their own issues of abuse sufficiently to be able to provide assistance to others. Leaders in particular must prioritize the safety of women and children, and make men accountable for the abuse they perpetrate.

The other source of mistrust in local resources and leaders relates to fears about confidentiality: people in rural communities are of course more intimately connected to each other than are people in urban centres. In order to overcome this distrust, rural professionals and leaders need to meet standards of professionalism regarding confidentiality. As well, they need to have resolved their own issues regarding violence. As a means to combat this shortcoming of alternative programs, a healing plan for workers in the field needs to be developed and funded.

The normalization of violence in Aboriginal communities is also an impediment to delivery of alternative programs. In Chapter 3, McGillivray and Comaskey found that band politics protecting the abuser, along with the normalization of violence, make service provision in rural communities difficult. Frequently band and reserve politics tend to protect the perpetrators of abuse, perhaps because the leaders themselves require healing and treatment or because the internal pain they experience regarding the intergenerational impact of abuse can be more easily managed by denying its occurrence. However, it is only through challenging the patterns of abuse that violence can be reduced or eliminated. The normalization of violence can only stop when community members are no longer willing to tolerate it within themselves and others.

McGillivray and Comaskey, in Chapter 3, also highlighted the contradiction between retributive justice, as it exists in mainstream models, and restitutive or restorative justice, which is the goal of Aboriginal-based systems. The Aboriginal women interviewed in their study expressed a lack of confidence in diversion projects because they felt that such programs failed to provide both punishment and treatment for their abusers. It may not only be women who prefer the mainstream system of justice; for some men, punishment in jail is preferable since they do not have to meet their victim and become directly accountable to them and their community. Since there is an automatic fallback to the mainstream justice system (results of the Aboriginal Ganootamaage Justice Service diversion project indicated that cases that do not meet the criteria for the program, or where the offender is not prepared to participate in a

Conclusion

healing plan, are reverted to the crown), offenders and victims are able to avoid participation in alternative systems. There is clearly a need for more education about alternative systems. Individuals need to consider the possibility that both punishment and treatment for offenders can be achieved through the community experience.

Another factor which can undermine the success of community-based treatment is that of solvent abuse. The Aboriginal Ganootamaage Justice Services of Winnipeg found that half of the solvent abusers who were referred to the program were not cooperative in their own healing. It is important to assess chemical dependency during the intake process. Part of the case plan might involve preparation for the diversion program through additional referral to a chemical dependency program. Participation in the diversion program could take place simultaneously with participation in a chemical dependency program and could be made contingent upon remaining in the chemical dependency program.

As well, the authors of Chapter 4 indicated that in all of the cases processed through the diversion project, only once did the victim participate in the healing process. It was suggested that because the majority of victims to date have been corporations and businesses, a lack of an individual victim has precluded the participation of victims in the healing process. However, if a diversion program is to articulate Aboriginal and community values it is imperative that both the victim and the offender be part of the healing circle. As victims cannot be forced into this type of participation, surrogate victims (victims of a similar crime) may be used to represent the victim. Such alternatives should be entertained as a holistic approach requires the direct involvement of the victim.

As previously mentioned, a number of cases that were referred to the diversion program were reverted back to the crown due to failure to attend the referral meeting, difficulties in locating the offender, and unsuccessful completion of the healing plan. Again, this may indicate that more preliminary work is necessary to explain the intricacies of the diversion project to offenders. Some individuals are not prepared for the diversion process, as they have been socialized towards greater familiarity and possibly greater regard for the mainstream system of justice.

In Chapter 5, the discussion of the blended programming available to Aboriginal sex offenders mentioned that only a small proportion of Aboriginal offenders chose to participate in the traditional healing program. Since, for some Aboriginal people, it is the first time they have had the opportunity to be exposed to cultural beliefs and traditions, their apprehension may be due to a fear of the unknown. The effects of colonization and institutional abuse may also have predisposed them to mistrust or deny their cultural teachings and to discount traditional ways.

As found by Ellerby, some communities do not support the return of the offender into the community. Part of the reason that communities do not support reintegration of sex offenders may be due to a lack of specific education and awareness regarding sexual offending. Open dialogue with communities and offenders may help to change this situation: current and potential offenders need help to realize that children are gifts from the Creator and that Aboriginal life and teachings give high priority to the preservation and protection of future generations. Communities can be vigilant about the detection of any inappropriate behaviour between adults and children. It is important to stress the responsibility of the community to inform all members when a sex offender is being re-introduced into the community. Reintegration and protection of children is a shared responsibility.

The author also mentioned that sweat-lodge ceremonies attended within the federal institution often contain non-sex offenders as well as sex offenders, creating fears for safety and limiting disclosures in sex offenders. Concern was voiced about requesting that Elders not allow non-sex offenders to participate in the ceremony. The responsibility for dictating who is allowed within institutional cultural ceremonies does not reside with the Elder. Rather, it is the program facilitators and administrators who must ensure the safety of group members and provide an environment conducive to open discussion and disclosure. Some concern was expressed about the participation of inauthentic and unhealthy Elders in the programs. Since Elders have been exposed to the same effects of colonization and intergenerational aspects of abuse as other Aboriginal people, healing treatment strategies and opportunities must also exist for the Elders prior to allowing them to help others in ceremonial practices and teachings.

In their discussion of the Ma Mawi Wi Chi Itata Family Violence Program, the authors of chapter 6 indicated that the post-program follow-up group within the institution was poorly attended and eventually was discontinued. This poor attendance was largely caused by time conflicts with other programs and employment. If follow-up groups are to be successful, administration has to endorse the program and provide the support required for inmates to attend them.

The Aboriginal people of North America faced the potential destruction of their culture and traditions with the onset of European conquest. This disruption of their way of life has had long-lasting repercussions. Generations of Aboriginal people have had to face racism, marginalization and isolation. Family and community, the essence of Aboriginal life, deteriorated as a sense of unity was lost and intergenerational abuse occurred. The isolation of reservations made them vulnerable to neglect, internal conflicts and violence. The strategies utilized to cope with the experiences have often had detrimental effects on individuals and the entire community. Addictions, suicide and violence are some of the maladaptive responses which developed as a result of the degeneration of community and family.

Despite these experiences, Aboriginal communities have survived assimilation and have managed to preserve many of their languages and customs. Although tenuous at times, cultural ties have remained. Increasingly, these ties are being nurtured and strengthened. Aboriginal communities are facing the challenge of teaching their own members about Aboriginal philosophies, traditions and ideologies. An understanding of the history of Aboriginal people is an essential part of these teachings. Knowledge of the effects of colonization provides individuals with a more comprehensive understanding of the process of culture building and the necessity of working to strengthen the Aboriginal community. The re-awakening of a sense of community has generated new interest in traditional ways and a search for various means to reintroduce these traditions to all generations of Aboriginal people.

More formal mechanisms to reintroduce these traditional values include workshops and courses on Aboriginal culture. However, the teachings can also be integrated into programs designed to treat community problems, such as violence. The participation of Elders is becoming an essential part of these initiatives; their input brings knowledge, wisdom and cultural teachings to younger generations. They can also become catalysts for change by modelling positive behaviours and attitudes. Workers, facilitators and the programs themselves can demonstrate the traditional values and encourage the reunification of community. Through their activities and organizations Aboriginal service providers are helping to rebuild their communities as they work to heal the families within these communities. It is important to remember that all individuals are members of the community, regardless of the position they choose or to which they are designated. Leaders within the Aboriginal community are not immune to the effects of social problems. Thus, their role can encompass both seeking and supporting solutions related to family violence.

Aboriginal people have also been teaching non-Aboriginal people about Aboriginal traditions. As with their own communities this is often done through courses in native studies and informational workshops. However, with the advent of community/academic collaboration, non-Aboriginal people are being exposed to Aboriginal culture though direct experience. These partnerships have the potential to generate respect for alternative perspectives and traditions. Recognizing that every culture has merit opens a venue for cultural exchange and the enrichment of life. A joining of collective experiences enables the achievement of solutions to complex social issues through the mobilization of a wide range of resources. Learning from one another cannot be accomplished in isolation: through combined efforts and common concerns and goals, empathy and a global sense of community can be generated.

Many of the collaborative efforts between non-Aboriginal and Aboriginal people have focused on addressing violence as an issue of significant concern in both communities. For years each community has worked independently to eradicate family violence. It is only recently that partnerships have been formed to work together on this social problem. Such combined effort represents an improved approach to ending family violence. Violence is not owned by one individual or group. Rather, exploring alternatives for victims of violence is a collective social responsibility that will be better accomplished through mutual problem solving and solution seeking. These partnerships not only hold the promise of resolution, but they open the way to greater social understanding and cooperation.

This volume presents a few of the innovative programs and studies being conducted within and by the Aboriginal community. Many of the programs described, and the volume itself, exemplify collaborative efforts between Aboriginal and non-Aboriginal communities, as well as between community-based organizations and academics. The work presented here emphasizes the conviction that Aboriginal people must continue to speak about and reflect on their experiences. It is through this process that alternatives to the mainstream criminal justice system will continue to develop. Through the interaction of those in the community with academics, expertise and knowledge can be shared, built and utilized to advance the process of healing the harm that has been done to Aboriginal families and communities. The success and respect that these projects have elicited from the community will build confidence and pave the way for this development.

References

Alexander, P.C., and Anderson, C.L. (1997). Incest, attachment, and developmental psychopathology. In D. Cicchetti and S.L. Toth (Eds.), *Rochester Symposium on Developmental Psychopathology, Developmental Perspectives on Trauma: Theory, Research, and Intervention*, (Vol. 8, pp. 343–377). Rochester, NY: University of Rochester Press.

Atkinson, R., Ellerby, L., Foss, H., and Cota, A. (June, 1991). *Psychological and Attitudinal Factors on Community Reintegration of Federally Incarcerated Offenders*. Calgary, Alberta: Canadian Psychological Association Annual Convention.

Badgley, R.F., Allard, H.A., and McCormick, N. (1984). *Sexual Offences Against Children* (J2– 50/1984E). Ottawa, ON: Department of Supply and Services.

Bandura, A. (1973). *Aggression: A Social Learning Analysis*. Englewood Cliffs, NJ: Prentice-Hall.

Berk, L. (1997). *Child Development*, (4th ed.). Needham Heights, Mass.: Allyn and Bacon.

Bonta, J., LaPrairie, C., and Wallace-Capretta, S. (1997). Risk prediction and re-offending: Aboriginal and non-aboriginal offenders. *Canadian Journal of Criminology, 39* (2), 127–144.

Bonta, J. Lipinski, S., and Martin, M. (1993). The characteristics of Aboriginal recidivists. *Canadian Journal of Criminology, 34* (3–4), 517–521.

Bopp, J., and Bopp, M. (1997). *Responding to sexual abuse: Developing a community based response team in Aboriginal communities*. Ottawa: Solicitor General Canada. Aboriginal Peoples Collections Technical Series #1.

Bopp, J., Bopp, M., Brown, L., and Lane, P. (1984). *The Sacred Tree*. Lethbridge, AB: Four Worlds Development Press.

Briere, J. (1992). *Child Abuse Trauma: Theory and Treatment of the Lasting Effects*. Newbury Park, CA: Sage.

Browne, A., and Finkelhor, D. (1986). Initial and long-term effects: A review of the research. In D. Finkelhor (Ed.), *A Sourcebook on Child Sexual Abuse*, (pp. 143–179). Beverly Hills, CA: Sage.

Calisco, J.A., and Milner, J.S. (1994). Childhood physical abuse, childhood social support, and adult child abuse potential. *Journal of Interpersonal Violence, 9* (1), 27–44.

Canadian Bar Association. (1989). *Locking Up Natives in Canada.* Toronto: The Association.

Canadian Justice Statistics (1994). *Statistics Canada Report: Family Violence in Canada, current national data.* June. Ottawa, ON: Department of Justice.

Canadian Panel on Violence Against Women. (1993). *Changing the Landscape: Ending Violence—Achieving Equality, The Final Report.* Ottawa: Supply and Services Canada.

Canadian Public Health Association (CPHA) (1994). *Violence in Society: A Public Health Perspective.* Ottawa: Canadian Public Health Association.

Chu, J.A., and Dill, D.L. (1990). Dissociative symptoms in relation to childhood physical and sexual abuse. *American Journal of Psychiatry, 147,* 887–892.

Coalition Opposed to Violence Against Women (COVAW). (1995). *Policy Statement.* Winnipeg: COVAW.

Cooper, M., Corrado, R., Karlberg, A.M., and Adams, L.P. (1992). Aboriginal suicide in British Columbia: An overview. *Canada's Mental Health, 40*(3), 19–23.

Correctional Service Canada. (1999). *Basic Facts About Federal Corrections.* Ottawa: Public Works and Government Services Canada.

Dexheimer Pharris, M., Resnick, M.D., and Blum, R.W. (1997). Protecting against hopelessness and suicidality in sexually abused American Indian adolescents. *Journal of Adolescent Health, 21,* 400–406.

Dutton, D.G., and Golant, S.K. (1995). *The Batterer: A Psychological Profile.* New York: Basic Books.

Dutton, D.G., and Hart, S.D. (1992). Risk markers for family violence in a federally incarcerated population. *International Journal of Law and Psychiatry, 15,* 101–112.

_____. (1994). Evidence for long-term, specific effects of childhood abuse and neglect on criminal behavior in men. *International Journal of Offender Therapy and Comparative Criminology, 36* (2), 129–137.

Dutton, D.G., and Holtzworth-Munroe, A. (1997). The role of early trauma in males who assault their wives. In D. Cicchetti and S.L. Toth (Eds.), *Rochester Symposium on Developmental Psychopathology, Developmental Perspective on Trauma: Theory, Research, and Intervention,* (Vol 8, pp. 379–401). Rochester NY: University of Rochester Press.

Ellerby, J. (1999). *Working with Aboriginal Elders: Understanding Aboriginal Elders and Healers and the Cultural Conflicts Involved in Health Care Agencies and Institutions.* Winnipeg, Manitoba: Earth Concepts. Available through www.earthconcepts.com

Ellerby, L. (1994). Community based treatment of Aboriginal sexual offenders: Facing realities and exploring possibilities. *Forum on Corrections Research, 6* (3), 23–25.

Ellerby, L., and Bedard, J. (2000). *Paths to Wellness: A Gathering of Communities*

Addressing Sexual Offending Behavior. Ottawa: Solicitor General Canada. Aboriginal Peoples Collections Technical Series.

Ellerby, L., Bedard, J., and Chartrand, S. (in press). Holism, wellness and spirituality: Moving from relapse prevention to healing. In D.R. Laws, S.M. Hudson and T. Ward (Eds.) *Remaking Relapse Prevention with Sex Offenders: A Sourcebook.* Beverley Hills, CA: Sage.

Ellerby, L., and Ellerby J. (1998). *Understanding and Evaluating the Role of Elders and Traditional Healing in Sexual Offender Treatment for Aboriginal Offenders.* Ottawa: Solicitor General Canada. Aboriginal Peoples Collections Technical Series # 18.

Ellerby, L., and Stonechild, J. (1998). Blending the traditional with the contemporary in the treatment of Aboriginal sexual offenders: A Canadian experience. In W.L. Marshall, Y.M. Fernandez, S.M. Hudson and T. Ward (Eds.), *Sourcebook of Treatment Programs for Sexual Offenders,* (pp. 399–415). New York: Plenum Press.

Ellis, R.H., and Milner, J.S. (1981). Child abuse and locus of control. *Psychological Reports, 48,* 507–510.

Fournier, S., and Crey, E. (1997). *Stolen From Our Embrace: The Abduction of First Nations Children and the Restoration of Aboriginal Communities.* Toronto: Douglas and McIntyre.

Frank, S. (1992). *Family Violence in Aboriginal Communities: A First Nations Report.* Victoria: Queen's Printer.

Freeman-Longo, R.E. (1986). The impact of sexual victimization on males. *Child Abuse and Neglect, 10,* 411–414.

Garbarino, J., and Kostelny, K. (1992). Child maltreatment as a community problem. *Child Abuse and Neglect, 16,* 455–464.

Gil, E. (1982). Institutional abuse of children in out-of-home care. *Child and Youth Services, 4,* (1–2), 7–13.

Gotowiec, A., and Beiser, M. (1993, 1994). Aboriginal children's mental health: Unique challenges. *Canada's Mental Health, 41*(4), 7–11.

Government of Canada, (1996). *Statistics Canada 1996 Census.* Ottawa: Statistics Canada.

Green, R. (1995). *Aboriginal Sentencing and Mediation Initiatives: The Sentencing Circle and Other Community Participation Models in Six Aboriginal Communities.* Unpublished LL.M. Thesis. Winnipeg: University of Manitoba.

Griffiths, C.T., and Verdun-Jones, S.N. (1994). *Canadian Criminal Justice.* Ottawa, ON: Harcourt- Brace.

Hall, L.A., Sachs, B., Rayens, M.K., and Lutenbacher, M. (1993). Childhood physical and sexual abuse: Their relationship with depressive symptoms in adulthood. *IMAGE: The Journal of Nursing Scholarship, 25*(4), 317–323.

Hamilton, A.C., and Sinclair, C.M. (1991). *The Justice System and Aboriginal People.* Winnipeg, MB: Queen's Printer.

Herring, R. (1989). The American Native family: Dissolution by coercion.

References

Journal of Multicultural Counselling and Development, 17 (1), 4–13.

Hirschbach, E. (1982). Children beyond reach? *Child and Youth Services, 4*, (1–2), 99–107.

Hofford, M. (1991). Family violence: Challenging cases for probation officers. *Federal Probation, 55* (3), 12–17.

Hollow Water First Nation Community Holistic Circle Healing. (1993). *Position Paper.* Hollow Water, MB: CHCH.

Hunter, J.A. (1991). A comparison of the psychosocial maladjustment of adult males and females sexually molested as children. *Journal of Interpersonal Violence, 6* (2), 205–217.

Kiyoshk, R. (1990). *Family Violence Research Report: Beyond Violence.* Vancouver: Helping Spirit Lodge.

Koniak-Griffin, D., and Lesser, J. (1996). The impact of childhood maltreatment on young mothers' violent behavior toward themselves and others. *Journal of Pediatric Nursing, 11*(5), 300–308.

LaFromboise, T.D., and Bigfoot, D.S. (1988). Cultural and cognitive considerations in the prevention of American Indian adolescent suicide. *Journal of Adolescence, 11*, 139–153.

LaPrairie, C. (1994). Victimization and family violence (Report 3). In *Seen But Not Heard: Native People in the Inner City.* Ottawa: Justice Canada.

_____. (1996). Community Justice or just communities? Aboriginal communities in search of justice. *Canadian Journal of Criminology, 37*(4), 521–545.

_____. (1996). *A State of Aboriginal Corrections.* Ottawa: Ministry of the Solicitor General Canada.

LaRocque, E. (1996). The colonization of the native woman scholar. In C. Miller and P. Chuchryk (eds.), *Women of the First Nations: Power, Wisdom, and Strength*, (pp. 11–18). Winnipeg: University of Manitoba Press.

_____. (1993). *Violence in Aboriginal Communities.* Report to the Aboriginal Justice Inquiry. Ottawa: Inquiry.

LeClair, M. (1996). *Profile of Aboriginal Sexual Offenders.* Ottawa: Correctional Service of Canada.

Lee, B. (1992). Colonization and community: Implications for first nations development. *Community Development Journal, 27* (3), 211–219.

MacEwan, K.E. (1994). Refining the intergenerational transmission hypothesis. *Journal of Interpersonal Violence, 9* (3), 350–365.

MacLeod, L. (1987). *Battered But Not Beaten: Preventing Wife Abuse in Canada.* Ottawa: Canadian Advisory Council on the Status of Women.

MacMillan, H.L., Fleming, J.E., Trocme, N., Boyle, M.H., Wong, M., Racine, Y.A., Beardslee, W.R., and Offord, D.R. (1997). Prevalence of child physical and sexual abuse in the community. *Journal of the American Medical Association, 278*(2), 131–135.

Manitoba. (1991). *Report of the Aboriginal Justice Inquiry of Manitoba.* Winnipeg: Queen's Printer.

_____. (1998). Winnipeg, MB: Manitoba Native Affairs Secretariat.

_____. (1999). Policy on First Nation government: Working in partnership.

Winnipeg, MB: Manitoba Northern Affairs Secretariat.

McFadden, E., and Ryan, P. (1991). Maltreatment in family foster homes: Dynamics and dimensions. *Child and Youth Services, 15*, (2), 209–231.

McGaa, E. (1990). *Mother Earth Spirituality: Native American Paths to Healing Ourselves and Our World.* San Francisco: Harper Collins.

McGillivray, A. (1999). Capturing childhood: The Indian child in the European imagination. In M. Freeman and A. Lewis (eds.), *Law and Literature,* (pp. 555–579). London: Oxford University Press.

_____. (1997). Therapies of freedom: The colonization of Aboriginal childhood. In A. McGillivray (ed.), *Governing Childhood,* (pp. 135–199). Aldershot: Dartmouth.

_____. (1987). Battered women: Models, policy, and prosecutorial discretion. *Canadian Journal of Family Law,6*(1), 15–43.

McGillivray, A., and Comaskey, B. (1999). *Black Eyes All of the Time: Intimate Violence, Aboriginal Women and the Justice System.* Toronto: University of Toronto Press.

Merry, S. (1997). Global human rights and local social movements in a legally plural world. *Canadian Journal of Law and Society, 12,* 247–271.

Meston, J. (1993). *Child Abuse and Neglect Prevention Programs.* The Vanier Institute of the Family. June.

Milner, J.S. (1988). An ego-strength scale for the Child Abuse Potential Inventory. *Journal of Family Violence, 3,* 151–162.

Milner, J.S., and Chilamkurti, C. (1991). Physical child abuse perpetrator characteristics: A review of the literature. *Journal of Interpersonal Violence, 6,* (3), 345–366.

Milner, J.S., Robertson, K.R., and Rogers, D.L. (1990). Childhood history of abuse and adult child abuse potential. *Journal of Family Violence, 5,* 15–34

Monture-Okanee, P.A. (1992). The roles and responsibilities of Aboriginal women: Reclaiming justice. *Saskatchewan Law Review, 56,* 237–266.

Motiuk, L., and Belcourt, R. (1996). *Homicide, Sexual, Robbery and Drug Offenders in Federal Corrections: End of 1995 Review.* Research Brief B-13, Ottawa: Correctional Service Canada.

Nabigon, H., and Mawhiney, A.M. (1996). Aboriginal theory: A Cree Medicine Wheel guide for healing First Nations. In F.J. Turner (Ed.), *Social Work Treatment: Interlocking Theoretical Approach* (4th ed.). New York, NY: The Free Press.

Native Women's Association of Canada. (1991). *Voices of Aboriginal Women: Aboriginal Women Speak Out About Violence.* Ottawa: Canadian Council on Social Development.

NDP Caucus Task Force. (1995). *Report on Violence Against Women.* Manitoba NDP.

Ontario Native Women's Association. (1989). *Breaking Free: A Proposal for Change to Aboriginal Family Violence.* Thunder Bay: The Association.

Pagelow, M.D. (1981). *Woman-battering.* Beverly Hills, CA: Sage.

References

Palmer, S., and Cooke, W. (1996). Understanding and countering racism with First Nations children in out-of-home care. *Child Welfare, 75* (6), 709–725.

Pedlar, D. (1991). *Domestic Violence Review into the Administration of Justice in Manitoba.* Winnipeg: Province of Manitoba.

Petric, N.D., Petric Olson, R.E., and Subotnik, L.S. (1994). Powerlessness and the need to control: The male abuser's dilemma. *Journal of Interpersonal Violence, 9* (2) 278–285.

Prairie Research Associates Inc. (1994). *Manitoba Spouse Abuse Tracking Project.* Ottawa: Department of Justice Canada.

Proulx, J., and Perrault, S. (1996). *An Evaluation of the Ma Mawi Wi Chi Itata Family Violence Program Stony Mountain Project.* Unpublished report. Available at: Ma Mawi Wi Chi Itata Family Violence Program, 5th floor, 338 Broadway, Winnipeg, MB.

Pynoos, R. S., and Nader, K. (1990). Children's exposure to violence and traumatic death. *Psychiatric Annals, 20*(6), 334–344.

Report of the Aboriginal Justice Inquiry of Manitoba (1996). *The Justice System and Aboriginal People.* (Volume 1). Winnipeg, MB: Queen's Printer.

Rodgers, K. (1994). Wife assault: The findings of a national survey. *Juristat Service Bulletin: Canadian Centre for Justice Statistics, 14* (9), 1–21.

Rogers, C.M., and Terry, T. (1984). Clinical interventions with boy victims of sexual abuse. In I. Stuart and J. Greer (Eds.), *Victims of Sexual Aggression* (pp. 91–104). New York: Van Nostrand Rienhold.

Ross, R. (1996). *Returning to the Teachings: Exploring Aboriginal Justice.* Toronto: Penguin Books.

_____. (1992). *Dancing With a Ghost: Exploring Indian Reality.* Markham, Ontario: Octopus Publishing Group.

Royal Commission on Aboriginal Peoples. (1996). *For Seven Generations* (Volume. 3). Ottawa, ON: Libraxus Inc.

_____. (1993). *Exploring the Options: Overview of the Third Round.* Ottawa: Supply and Services Canada.

_____. (1992). *Community Council Project.* Toronto, ON: Aboriginal Legal Services of Toronto.

Sanders, B., and Giolas, M.H. (1991). Dissociation and childhood trauma in psychologically disturbed adolescents. *American Journal of Psychiatry, 148,* 50–54.

Schulman, Judge P.W. (1997). *A Study of Domestic Violence and the Justice System in Manitoba: Commission of Inquiry into the Deaths of Rhonda Lavoie and Roy Lavoie.* Winnipeg: Province of Manitoba.

Shkilnyk, A.M. (1985). *A Poison Stronger Than Love: The Destruction of an Ojibway Community.* New Haven, CN: Yale University Press.

Smart, C. (1989). *Feminism and the Power of Law.* London: Routledge.

Statistics Canada. (1994). *Canadian Crime Statistics.* Ottawa: Canadian Centre for Justice Statistics.

_____. (1991). *Adult Corrections Survey.* Ottawa: Canadian Centre for Justice

Statistics.

Steele, B.F. (1987). Psychodynamic factors in child abuse. In R.E. Helfer and C.H. Kempe (Eds.) *The Battered Child* (4th ed., pp. 81–114). Chicago: University of Chicago Press.

Strickland, C.J. (1997). Suicide among American Indian, Alaskan Native, and Canadian Aboriginal youth: advancing the research agenda. *International Journal of Mental Health, 25*(4), 11–32.

Thomlinson, B., Erickson, N., and Packo, R. (1996). A determination of reported cases of family violence and violence against women. In J. Oakes and R. Riewe (Eds.), *Issues in the North,* (pp. 17–20). Edmonton, AB: Canadian Circumpolar Institute.

Thomlinson, E.B., Erickson, N., and Cook, M. (2000). Family violence: How can we tell what is happening? In J. Oakes, R. Riewe, S. Koolage, L. Simpson, and N. Schuster (Eds.), *Aboriginal Health, Identity and Resources,* (pp. 70–82). University of Manitoba, Winnipeg: Winnipeg Native Studies Press.

Thompson Crisis Centre. (1988). *Aboriginal Justice Inquiry Hearings.* Thompson, MB, September 21.

Timpson, J. (1995). Four decades of literature on Native Canadian child welfare: Changing themes. *Child Welfare, 74* (3), 525–546.

Tomkiewicz, S. (1984). Violence and negligence towards children and adolescents in institutions. *Child Abuse and Neglect, 8,* (3), 319–335.

Towberman, D.B. (1994). Psychosocial antecedents of chronic delinquency. *Journal of Offender Rehabilitation, 21,* (1–2), 151–164.

Turner, J. (1995). Saskatchewan responds to family violence. In Valverde, McLeod and Johnson (Eds.), *Wife Assault and the Canadian Criminal Justice System.* Toronto: University of Toronto Centre of Criminology.

Ursel, J. (1998). *Lavoie Inquiry Implementation Committee: Final Report.* (Unpublished.) Winnipeg.

_____. (1991). Considering the impact of the battered women's movement on the state: The example of Manitoba. In E. Comack and S. Brickey, (eds.), *The Social Basis of Law,* 2nd ed., (pp. 261–288). Halifax: Fernwood.

Waldram, J.B. (1993). Aboriginal spirituality: Symbolic healing in Canadian prisons. *Culture, Medicine, and Psychiatry, 17* (3), 345–362.

Waldram, J.B., and Wong, S. (1995). Group therapy of Aboriginal offenders in a Canadian forensic psychiatric facility. *American Indian and Alaska Native Mental Health Research, 6* (2), 34–56.

Warry, W. (1998). *Unfinished Dreams: Community Healing and the Reality of Aboriginal Self-Government.* Toronto: University of Toronto Press.

Weeks, R., and Widom, C.S. (1998). Self-reports of early childhood victimization among incarcerated adult male felons. *Journal of Interpersonal Violence, 13* (3), 346–361.

Williams, S., Vallee, S., and Staubi, B. (1997). *Aboriginal Sexual Offenders: Melding Spiritual Healing with Cognitive-Behavioral Treatment.* Ottawa: Correctional Service Canada.

Wolfe, D.A., Edwards, B., Manion, I., and Koverola, C. (1988). Early interventions for parents at risk of child abuse and neglect: A preliminary investigation. *Journal of Consulting and clinical Psychology, 56*, 40–47.

Wyse, M. and Thomasson, K. (1999). A perspective on sexual offender treatment for Native Americans. In A.D. Lewis (Ed.), *Cultural Diversity in Sexual Abuser Treatment: Issues and Approaches*, (pp. 83–107). Brandon, Vermont: Safer Society Press.

York, G. (1990). *The Dispossessed*. Toronto, ON: Little, Brown, and Company.

Young, R.E., Bergandi, T.A., and Titus, T.G. (1994). Comparison of the effects of sexual abuse on male and female latency-aged children. *Journal of Interpersonal Violence, 9* (3), 291–306.

Zylberberg, P. (1991). Who should make child protection decisions for the Native community? *Windsor Yearbook to Access to Justice, 11*, 74–103.

Hurting and Healing: A Series on Intimate Violence

The Hurting and Healing series on intimate violence is a project of RESOLVE a tri-provincial research network on family violence. RESOLVE (Research and Education for Solutions to Violence and Abuse) is committed to conducting and encouraging pragmatic program and policy based research in partnership with community agencies. We have offices in Winnipeg, Saskatoon and Calgary and partnerships with seven prairie universities and a broad range of community based agencies in each province. Our Hurting and Healing book series reflects the philosophy of our organization with partner editors and contributors from the university and the community.

The increasing disclosure of violence in families and intimate relations poses many questions for practitioners and policy-makers. What is the most effective way to intervene and stop the intergenerational cycle of violence? Does criminalization help or make matters worse? Can family violence offenders be rehabilitated? Most importantly; How can we prevent the violence from happening in the first place? Over the years our research projects have grappled with these issues. In the Hurting and Healing series we will be sharing the results of some of our studies with you. We hope that our books will be useful to practitioners and researchers alike.

We are very proud of our first volume and hope you will look for the next two books in our series:

Spring 2001 Volume 2
Pieces of the Puzzle: Strategies for Change in Child Sexual Abuse
edited by Diane Hiebert-Murphy (Social Work, University of Manitoba) and Linda Burnside (Winnipeg Child and Family Services)
140pp $15.95.

Spring 2002 Volume 3
Women Abused by Intimate Partners: Challenges and Solutions
edited by Leslie Tutty (Social Work, University of Calgary) and Carolyn Goard (Sheriff King Family Support Centre, Calgary)
140pp $15.95.